The People's Amendments

James R. Whitfield

Published by Fiel LLC, 2024.

THE PEOPLE'S AMENDMENTS

First edition. November 14, 2024.

ISBN: 979-8230034896

Written by James R. Whitfield.

Table of Contents

The Living Document: Introduction to Constitutional Change

The United States Constitution stands unique among governing documents not just for its remarkable longevity, but for its built-in capacity for change. While many nations have cycled through multiple constitutions or complete governmental overhauls, Americans have chosen instead to adapt their founding charter through a process of careful amendment, allowing it to evolve alongside the nation it serves. This evolutionary approach has created what legal scholars often call a "living document," one that breathes and grows with the American people while maintaining its essential character.

When the delegates to the Constitutional Convention gathered in Philadelphia during the sweltering summer of 1787, they recognized that no document could perfectly anticipate the needs of future generations. James Madison, often called the Father of the Constitution, wrote extensively about the necessity of having a mechanism for constitutional change. In Federalist No. 43, he argued that the amendment process should be neither too easy, which would make the Constitution too mutable, nor too difficult, which would render necessary changes impossible. The solution they crafted in Article V created a demanding but achievable path to constitutional change, requiring both congressional and state approval for any modification.

This careful balance has proven remarkably successful. Over more than two centuries, Americans have ratified only 27 amendments to their Constitution, each representing a hard fought victory for democratic change. These amendments tell the story of America itself, chronicling the nation's growth from a fledgling republic to a modern superpower, its struggles with slavery and civil rights, its expansion of democratic participation, and its ongoing efforts to perfect its governmental systems. Each amendment emerged from specific historical circumstances, driven by social movements, catalyzed by cultural changes, and shaped by political compromise.

The process of amending the Constitution has never been easy, nor was it meant to be. The requirement for a two thirds vote in both houses of Congress, followed by ratification by three fourths of state legislatures, ensures that only proposals with broad and deep support can succeed. This high bar has meant that for every successfully ratified amendment, many more proposals have failed. Since 1789, more than 11,000 amendment proposals have been introduced in Congress, but only 33 have achieved the necessary congressional supermajority, and only 27 have successfully navigated the full ratification process.

These successful amendments cluster around distinct historical periods, reflecting moments when the American people faced unprecedented challenges or underwent dramatic social change. The first ten amendments, known collectively as the Bill of Rights, came immediately after ratification, responding to Anti Federalist concerns about individual liberty. The Reconstruction Amendments (13th, 14th, and 15th) emerged from the Civil War, fundamentally reshaping American citizenship and federal power. The Progressive Era brought four amendments in quick succession, expanding democracy through direct election of senators, income tax, women's suffrage, and Prohibition. The latter half of the 20th century saw amendments addressing presidential succession, voting rights, and governmental procedures.

Understanding these amendments requires more than just reading their text. Each represents the culmination of complex social movements, political battles, and cultural shifts. The Nineteenth Amendment's guarantee of women's suffrage, for instance, cannot be fully appreciated without understanding the seventy year struggle of the women's rights movement, from Seneca Falls to the final dramatic ratification battle in Tennessee. Similarly, the Fourth Amendment's protections against unreasonable searches and seizures take on new meaning when viewed through the lens of colonial resistance to British writs of assistance.

The impact of constitutional amendments extends far beyond their immediate historical context. Through judicial interpretation and practical application, amendments often develop meanings and implications their authors could never have anticipated. The First Amendment's protection of "freedom of speech" now applies to internet communication and campaign finance. The Fourth Amendment's restrictions on government searches must be constantly reinterpreted for an age of digital surveillance and automated data collection. The Fourteenth Amendment's guarantee of "equal protection of the laws" has become the constitutional foundation for civil rights advances its drafters never explicitly considered.

This process of constitutional evolution through amendment represents a remarkable achievement in democratic governance. It has allowed the American constitutional system to adapt to dramatic social, technological, and cultural changes while maintaining fundamental continuity. The amendment process has provided a peaceful, legal mechanism for revolutionary change, from abolishing slavery to guaranteeing women's right to vote. It has allowed each generation of Americans to participate in shaping their fundamental law, while ensuring that changes reflect broad national consensus rather than temporary majorities.

Yet the amendment process has not been without controversy or criticism. Some argue that the requirements for amendment are too stringent, pointing to the difficulty of achieving needed reforms in an increasingly polarized political environment. Others contend that certain amendments, particularly the Fourteenth, have been interpreted too broadly by courts, effectively amending the Constitution through judicial decision rather than the formal amendment process. These debates themselves reflect the ongoing vitality of constitutional discourse in American life.

As we examine each amendment in detail throughout this book, we will see how they collectively tell the story of American democracy: its achievements, its struggles, its failures, and its ongoing evolution. We will meet the activists who fought for change, the politicians who shaped compromise, the judges who interpreted new provisions, and the ordinary citizens whose lives were transformed. Through their stories, we will understand how the Constitution has remained both permanent and adaptable, providing stability while accommodating change. This is the story of how Americans have repeatedly risen to the challenge of remaking their fundamental law to better realize the promise of democracy for all people.

Birth of a Nation's Laws: The Constitutional Convention

The Constitutional Convention of 1787 marked a pivotal moment in American history, bringing together the nation's most prominent leaders to craft a new system of government. Meeting in the Pennsylvania State House (now Independence Hall) during a sweltering Philadelphia summer, fifty-five delegates from twelve states embarked on what would become a transformative four-month journey to create the United States Constitution.

The path to the Convention began with growing recognition that the Articles of Confederation, America's first governing document, had proven inadequate for the young nation's needs. Under the Articles, states maintained nearly complete sovereignty, Congress lacked power to regulate commerce or collect taxes, and unanimous consent was required for any significant changes. These limitations had led to economic chaos, diplomatic weakness, and increasing discord between states.

Initially called simply to revise the Articles, the Convention's delegates quickly concluded that a complete overhaul was necessary. Virginia's Governor Edmund Randolph opened proceedings by presenting what became known as the Virginia Plan, drafted largely by James Madison. This ambitious proposal called for a strong national government with proportional representation based on population, a dramatic departure from the Articles' one state, one vote system.

The smaller states, led by New Jersey's William Paterson, pushed back with their own plan maintaining equal representation regardless of size. This fundamental conflict threatened to derail the entire Convention until Roger Sherman of Connecticut proposed the Great Compromise: a bicameral legislature with proportional representation in the House and equal state representation in the Senate.

This spirit of pragmatic compromise would prove essential throughout the Convention. The delegates navigated numerous contentious issues through careful negotiation and mutual accommodation. The question of slavery proved particularly challenging, leading to morally fraught compromises like counting three fifths of the enslaved population for representation and protecting the slave trade from federal interference for twenty years.

The Convention's delegates represented America's political elite, including future presidents George Washington and James Madison, future Supreme Court Chief Justice John Jay, and elder statesman Benjamin Franklin. Their average age was forty-two, though Franklin at eighty-one and Jonathan Dayton at twenty-six marked the extremes. Most were well-educated and prosperous, with backgrounds in law, business, or plantation agriculture.

Notable absences included Thomas Jefferson and John Adams, both serving as ambassadors abroad, and Patrick Henry, who famously refused to attend, saying he "smelt a rat." Several delegates left during the proceedings, and three refused to sign the final document. Rhode Island boycotted the Convention entirely, earning the nickname "Rogue Island" from its frustrated neighbors.

The Convention operated under strict secrecy, with windows closed despite the summer heat to prevent eavesdropping. This confidentiality, maintained by all participants, allowed for frank discussion and willingness to change positions. James Madison's detailed notes, published years later, provide our primary window into the debates and negotiations that shaped the Constitution.

Beyond specific provisions, the Convention grappled with fundamental questions about the nature of democracy and government. How could liberty be preserved while ensuring sufficient authority for effective governance? How could majority rule be balanced with minority rights? How could power be properly divided between state and national governments? Their solutions, while imperfect, created a remarkably durable framework for American democracy.

The final document represented neither complete victory nor defeat for any faction. As Benjamin Franklin observed when urging unanimous support, "I confess that there are several parts of this Constitution which I do not at present approve, but I am not sure I shall never approve them." This recognition that compromise was necessary for progress would prove essential for ratification.

The Convention's work concluded on September 17, 1787, with thirty-nine delegates signing the Constitution. However, their achievement remained uncertain until ratification by the required nine states, a process that would take nearly two years and generate intense debate through the Federalist Papers and other political discourse.

The Convention established several crucial precedents for American governance. It demonstrated that fundamental political change could occur through peaceful deliberation rather than violence. It showed how competing interests could be reconciled through careful institutional design. Perhaps most importantly, it created a system flexible enough to accommodate future change through the amendment process.

The delegates' decision to begin the Constitution with "We the People" rather than "We the States" signaled a revolutionary understanding of political authority flowing from the people themselves. This principle would prove essential for the document's legitimacy and adaptability over time. Though the Convention's immediate product was imperfect, particularly in its accommodation of slavery, it created mechanisms for its own improvement through amendment and interpretation.

The Convention's success relied heavily on the personal relationships and shared experiences of its participants. Many delegates had worked together during the Revolution or under the Articles of Confederation. Despite their differences, they shared a common commitment to creating a workable system of republican government, something few believed possible on such a grand scale.

The Constitution they produced has proven remarkably durable, in part because it focused on creating institutions and processes rather than prescribing detailed policies. The Convention established broad principles and frameworks, leaving future generations to work out specific applications through legislation, judicial interpretation, and constitutional amendment.

Understanding the Constitutional Convention provides essential context for studying subsequent amendments. The delegates' debates foreshadowed many of the challenges and controversies that would drive constitutional change, from federal-state relations to individual rights to the scope of democratic participation. Their work created both the foundation for American government and the tools for its evolution through amendment.

A Promise of Rights: The Path to the Bill of Rights

The journey toward the Bill of Rights began even before the ink dried on the Constitution. During the ratification debates, Anti-Federalists voiced grave concerns about the Constitution's lack of explicit protections for individual liberties. These critics, including prominent figures like George Mason and Patrick Henry, argued that without clear restrictions on federal power, the new government could become as tyrannical as the British monarchy they had fought to escape.

James Madison, initially skeptical of the need for a Bill of Rights, came to recognize that securing these protections was both politically necessary and philosophically sound. During his campaign for the First Congress, he promised his Virginia constituents that he would champion a Bill of Rights if elected. This pledge proved crucial to his victory and set the stage for one of the most significant constitutional developments in American history.

The process of crafting the Bill of Rights drew heavily on existing state constitutions and the English Bill of Rights of 1689. Virginia's Declaration of Rights, drafted by George Mason, provided a particularly influential model. Madison carefully studied these precedents while also considering the specific concerns raised during ratification debates. His initial proposal to Congress included seventeen amendments, which he suggested should be integrated throughout the Constitution's text rather than added as a separate list.

Congress began debating Madison's proposals in June 1789. The House of Representatives appointed a select committee, including Madison, to refine the amendments. Through careful negotiation and revision, the seventeen proposals were consolidated into twelve amendments. Some of Madison's original suggestions were significantly altered or eliminated, including provisions regarding state governments and civil jury trials.

The debate in Congress revealed differing views about the purpose and scope of these protections. Some members wanted to include additional rights, while others feared that listing specific rights might imply that unlisted rights were unprotected. This concern led to the inclusion of what would become the Ninth Amendment, explicitly stating that the enumeration of certain rights should not be construed to deny others retained by the people.

The proposed amendments faced varying levels of opposition. Some Federalists still considered them unnecessary, while Anti-Federalists argued they didn't go far enough in restricting federal power. The amendments' supporters successfully argued that they would provide essential safeguards without undermining the new government's effectiveness. By September 1789, both houses of Congress had approved twelve amendments to be sent to the states for ratification.

The ratification process in the states proved more complicated than many had anticipated. Some states quickly approved the amendments, while others engaged in lengthy debates. Several states initially rejected some amendments while accepting others. The process highlighted continuing tensions between federal and state authority, as well as different regional perspectives on rights and liberties.

Of the twelve amendments submitted to the states, only ten achieved ratification in 1791. The first proposed amendment, dealing with congressional apportionment, was never ratified. The second, regarding congressional pay raises, would finally be ratified in 1992 as the Twenty-seventh Amendment. The ten successful amendments became known as the Bill of Rights, fundamentally shaping American concepts of liberty and justice.

The impact of the Bill of Rights was not immediately apparent. Initially, these protections applied only to the federal government, not to state actions. Many of the rights remained relatively dormant in judicial terms until the twentieth century, when the Supreme Court began applying them to the states through the Fourteenth Amendment's due process clause. This process of incorporation dramatically expanded the Bill of Rights' practical significance.

The creation of the Bill of Rights established important precedents for future constitutional amendments. It demonstrated that the Constitution could be improved through careful deliberation and consensus-building. The process also showed how public debate and political pressure could lead to significant constitutional change, a pattern that would repeat throughout American history.

Madison's role in securing the Bill of Rights represented a remarkable evolution in his thinking about constitutional rights. His initial skepticism gave way to a deep appreciation for the value of explicitly protected liberties. This transformation reflected broader changes in American political thought about the relationship between government power and individual rights.

The Bill of Rights emerged from a specific historical context but transcended it to become a cornerstone of American democracy. Its provisions reflected both ancient principles of English common law and Enlightenment ideals about natural rights. The amendments addressed immediate concerns about potential government overreach while establishing enduring principles of liberty and justice.

The success of the Bill of Rights demonstrated the wisdom of building flexibility into the constitutional system. The amendment process provided a peaceful means of addressing the Constitution's perceived shortcomings without undermining its basic framework. This ability to adapt while maintaining stability would prove crucial to the Constitution's longevity.

The legacy of the Bill of Rights extends far beyond American shores. Its principles have influenced constitutional developments worldwide and continue to inspire movements for human rights and democracy. The amendments serve as a reminder that constitutional rights are not simply granted from above but emerge from the persistent demands of citizens for protection of their liberties.

Speaking Truth to Power: First Amendment's Origins

The First Amendment stands as perhaps the most celebrated and frequently invoked of all constitutional protections, but its path to ratification involved complex debates about the nature of liberty in the new republic. When James Madison introduced his initial proposals for the Bill of Rights, the provisions that would become the First Amendment were actually spread across several different sections. The consolidation of these fundamental freedoms - religion, speech, press, assembly, and petition - into a single amendment reflected both practical considerations and a growing understanding of how these rights reinforced each other.

Religious freedom was particularly contentious during the drafting process. Many states still maintained official churches, and there were fierce disagreements about whether the amendment should simply prohibit a national establishment of religion or go further in protecting religious practice. Madison's original language borrowed heavily from Virginia's Statute for Religious Freedom, which he had helped Thomas Jefferson shepherd through the state legislature. The final wording - "Congress shall make no law respecting an establishment of religion, or prohibiting the free exercise thereof" - represented a careful compromise that both prevented federal interference with state religious establishments and protected individual religious liberty.

The protection of free speech emerged from the American experience with British censorship and sedition laws. During the colonial period, criticism of government authorities could result in severe punishment, and revolutionary leaders had firsthand experience with the suppression of political dissent. However, even supporters of free speech protections debated their exact scope. Some argued for absolute protection of political speech while accepting limitations on other forms of expression. Others worried that too much freedom might lead to social disorder or moral decay.

Freedom of the press held special significance for the founding generation. Newspapers had played a crucial role in spreading revolutionary ideas and coordinating resistance to British rule. Printers faced prosecution for seditious libel when they published material critical of colonial authorities. The founders understood that a free press was essential to democratic governance, allowing citizens to share information and opinions about public affairs. Yet they also grappled with questions about whether freedom of the press included protection for false or malicious publications.

The rights of assembly and petition were closely linked in the founders' minds to the broader concept of popular sovereignty. The ability to gather peacefully and present grievances to government officials had deep roots in English common law. Colonial Americans had exercised these rights extensively during the resistance to British policy, through meetings, committees of correspondence, and petitions to Parliament. The First Amendment enshrined these traditional rights while connecting them to newer concepts of democratic participation.

Early interpretations of the First Amendment were relatively narrow. Like the rest of the Bill of Rights, it initially applied only to actions by the federal government. States remained free to restrict speech, press, and religious freedom as they saw fit. The Supreme Court's first significant First Amendment case didn't come until 1919, in Schenck v. United States, which established the "clear and present danger" test for limiting speech.

The expansion of First Amendment protections came gradually through the twentieth century. The Supreme Court began applying First Amendment restrictions to state governments through the Fourteenth Amendment's due process clause. Cases involving labor activists, religious minorities, civil rights protesters, and anti-war demonstrators helped define the modern understanding of First

Amendment rights. The Court developed tests for different types of speech restrictions and refined its approach to religious establishment and free exercise claims.

The debate over religious freedom has evolved significantly since the First Amendment's ratification. Early concerns about government-established churches gave way to more nuanced questions about religious expression in public life, government funding of religious institutions, and accommodations for religious practice. The Supreme Court has struggled to balance the sometimes competing demands of the establishment and free exercise clauses.

Freedom of speech has expanded far beyond what the founders might have envisioned. The Court has extended protection to symbolic speech, commercial speech, and even some forms of offensive or controversial expression. At the same time, certain categories of speech - such as true threats, incitement to imminent lawless action, and obscenity - remain outside First Amendment protection. The rise of mass media and digital communication has created new challenges for applying First Amendment principles.

Press freedom has faced particular challenges in the modern era. The decline of traditional newspapers and the rise of online media have raised questions about who qualifies as "the press" for First Amendment purposes. Issues of national security, privacy rights, and the role of social media platforms have complicated discussions about press freedom and responsibility.

The rights of assembly and petition have taken on new significance in an age of mass protest movements and online organizing. Courts have had to balance these fundamental rights against public safety concerns and property rights. The internet has created new forms of assembly and petition while raising questions about how traditional First Amendment protections apply in digital spaces.

Throughout its history, the First Amendment has demonstrated remarkable adaptability to changing social and technological conditions. Its fundamental principles have been applied to situations the founders could never have imagined, while maintaining their essential character as bulwarks against government overreach and guarantors of democratic discourse.

The First Amendment's journey from controversial proposal to cornerstone of American democracy reflects broader themes in constitutional development. It shows how carefully crafted compromises can provide enduring principles for protecting essential liberties. Its evolution demonstrates the vital role of judicial interpretation in adapting constitutional protections to new circumstances while preserving their core purpose.

Today, the First Amendment continues to generate intense debate about its proper interpretation and application. Questions about hate speech, campaign finance, religious exemptions, and internet regulation challenge courts and citizens to consider how these fundamental freedoms should operate in contemporary society. Yet the amendment's basic promise - that government should not interfere with the essential liberties of conscience, expression, and democratic participation - remains as vital as ever.

Arms and Democracy: The Second Amendment Story

Few constitutional provisions have generated as much passionate debate as the Second Amendment. Its twenty seven words about the right to bear arms have sparked centuries of discussion about the relationship between individual rights, collective security, and the role of government in regulating weapons. The amendment's origins lie in the complex interplay between English legal traditions, colonial experiences, and the founders' vision for their new republic.

The right to bear arms had deep roots in English common law, where it was connected to both individual self defense and collective security through citizen militias. The English Bill of Rights of 1689 explicitly protected Protestant subjects' right to arm themselves, though this right was not unlimited. Colonial Americans inherited this legal tradition but adapted it to their circumstances, where firearms were essential tools for both personal protection and community defense.

The American Revolution transformed colonists' understanding of armed citizenship. The war began when British authorities attempted to seize colonial weapons stores, and citizen militias played a crucial role in the fight for independence. Many revolutionary leaders came to see an armed citizenry as an essential safeguard against tyranny. Yet they also recognized the potential dangers of unorganized armed groups, as demonstrated by events like Shays' Rebellion.

When the Constitutional Convention met in 1787, military matters were a major concern. The new Constitution gave Congress significant powers over military affairs, including authority to raise armies and regulate militias. This centralization of military power alarmed many Anti Federalists, who feared it could lead to standing armies that might threaten liberty. The Second Amendment emerged as part of the compromise that secured ratification of the Constitution.

James Madison's initial draft of what would become the Second Amendment explicitly connected the right to bear arms with military service, while also including language about conscientious objection. The final version emerged through extensive debate and revision in Congress. The result was characteristically concise but ambiguous: "A well regulated Militia, being necessary to the security of a free State, the right of the people to keep and bear Arms, shall not be infringed."

Early interpretations of the Second Amendment focused primarily on its relationship to militia service. State courts generally recognized broad authority to regulate individual weapon possession while protecting militia related rights. The first major Supreme Court case addressing the Second Amendment, United States v. Miller in 1939, upheld federal regulation of sawed off shotguns because they lacked a reasonable relationship to militia service.

The nineteenth century saw significant developments in both firearms technology and gun regulation. The introduction of mass produced revolvers and repeating rifles transformed both military and civilian weapons. States and cities enacted various gun control measures, particularly in response to urban violence. Courts generally upheld these regulations as compatible with Second Amendment rights.

The debate over the Second Amendment's meaning intensified during the twentieth century. The National Rifle Association, founded after the Civil War as a marksmanship organization, became increasingly focused on opposing gun control measures. Scholars and activists developed competing interpretations of the amendment's text and history. Some emphasized its connection to militia service, while others argued for a broader individual right to bear arms.

A major shift in Second Amendment interpretation came with the Supreme Court's 2008 decision in District of Columbia v. Heller. The

Court held for the first time that the Second Amendment protects an individual right to possess firearms for lawful purposes such as self defense in the home, independent of militia service. This landmark ruling was followed by McDonald v. Chicago in 2010, which applied this individual right to state and local governments through the Fourteenth Amendment.

However, the Court emphasized that this individual right is not unlimited. The Heller decision explicitly recognized the validity of many traditional forms of gun regulation, including prohibitions on possession by felons and the mentally ill, restrictions on carrying weapons in sensitive places like schools and government buildings, and laws imposing conditions on commercial gun sales.

The modern debate over gun rights and regulation continues to evolve. Mass shootings have intensified calls for stricter gun control measures, while gun rights advocates argue that such restrictions infringe on constitutional rights and fail to prevent violence. Courts have had to address questions about assault weapons bans, large capacity magazine restrictions, concealed carry permits, and other regulatory measures.

Technological changes continue to raise new Second Amendment questions. The development of 3D printed firearms, smart guns, and other innovations challenges traditional regulatory frameworks. Courts and legislators must consider how Second Amendment principles apply to these new technologies while balancing public safety concerns.

The Second Amendment's history reflects broader themes in American constitutional development. It shows how constitutional provisions can acquire new meanings as social conditions and understandings change. It demonstrates the ongoing tension between individual rights and public safety, and between federal power and state authority. Perhaps most importantly, it illustrates how constitutional interpretation involves not just legal analysis but fundamental questions about the nature of American democracy and the proper balance between liberty and security.

The debate over the Second Amendment seems unlikely to be resolved definitively anytime soon. Like many constitutional provisions, it requires each generation to strike its own balance between competing values and interests. What remains constant is its place at the center of enduring American discussions about rights, responsibilities, and the role of government in ensuring both freedom and safety.

Quartering and Liberty: Third Amendment's War Origins

The Third Amendment, though rarely litigated in modern times, emerged from one of the most contentious practices of British colonial rule: the forced quartering of soldiers in private homes. This imposition of military presence into domestic life represented a tangible symbol of royal authority that colonists found particularly galling, and its prohibition became a fundamental element of American constitutional rights.

The practice of quartering troops had deep roots in English history. Medieval kings had long claimed the right to house soldiers in private dwellings, though this power was gradually restricted through various legal reforms. The English Bill of Rights of 1689 limited quartering by requiring Parliamentary authorization, but these protections didn't extend fully to the colonies.

The French and Indian War (1754-1763) brought the quartering issue to the forefront of colonial grievances. As British forces arrived in North America in unprecedented numbers, colonial assemblies faced increasing pressure to provide for their housing. The Quartering Act of 1765, followed by a stricter version in 1774, required colonial assemblies to provide barracks and supplies for British troops. When barracks proved insufficient, soldiers could be quartered in public houses, inns, and as a last resort, in private homes.

This forced hospitality created numerous practical and symbolic problems. Beyond the immediate financial burden of feeding and housing soldiers, colonists resented the intrusion into their domestic sphere. The presence of armed soldiers in private homes undermined the English tradition of the home as castle, while also providing the Crown with a means of surveillance and intimidation. The quartering of troops became a powerful symbol of British oppression, listed among the grievances in the Declaration of Independence.

New York City became a particular flashpoint for quartering disputes. When the New York assembly refused to fully comply with quartering requirements in 1766, Parliament suspended its legislative authority until it acquiesced. This constitutional crisis highlighted the broader conflict between colonial self-government and imperial authority.

During the Revolutionary War, both sides faced quartering challenges. The Continental Congress, while denouncing British quartering practices, had to handle the housing needs of its own troops. George Washington consistently sought to avoid forcible quartering, recognizing its political sensitivity. However, military necessity sometimes required imposing on civilian households, though usually with compensation.

When the Constitutional Convention met in 1787, the quartering issue received relatively little attention. The new Constitution's provisions regarding military powers focused more on questions of raising armies and controlling militias. However, during the ratification debates, Anti-Federalists raised concerns about potential military impositions under the new government.

The Third Amendment emerged as part of the Bill of Rights package championed by James Madison. Its final text was straightforward: "No Soldier shall, in time of peace be quartered in any house, without the consent of the Owner, nor in time of war, but in a manner to be prescribed by law." This language reflected both the absolute prohibition in peacetime and the qualified restriction during war.

Unlike many other Bill of Rights provisions, the Third Amendment generated relatively little debate during ratification. Its principles commanded broad support, and its limitations seemed clear. The amendment effectively ended the practice of peacetime quartering in the United States, while establishing constitutional parameters for any wartime necessity.

The Third Amendment has seen limited judicial interpretation, primarily because the federal government has generally avoided quartering troops in private homes. The most significant case, Engblom v. Carey (1982), involved New York corrections officers who were evicted from their staff housing during a strike. The Second Circuit Court of Appeals ruled that the Third Amendment protected the officers from being displaced by National Guard troops, marking the first time a court found a Third Amendment violation.

Despite its narrow modern application, the Third Amendment embodies important constitutional principles. It represents one of the earliest recognitions of privacy rights in American law, establishing the home as a sphere protected from government intrusion. This concept has influenced interpretation of other constitutional provisions, particularly the Fourth Amendment's protections against unreasonable searches and seizures.

The amendment also reflects broader themes about civilian-military relations in American society. By limiting military intrusion into domestic life, it helps maintain the separation between civilian and military spheres that the founders considered essential to republican government. This principle remains relevant to modern debates about military power and civil liberties.

The Third Amendment's prohibition on quartering has shaped military practices throughout American history. During the Civil War, both Union and Confederate forces generally avoided forcible quartering, instead establishing separate camps and barracks. This pattern continued through subsequent conflicts, with the military developing independent housing systems rather than imposing on civilian homes.

In modern times, the Third Amendment's principles have found new relevance in discussions of government surveillance and privacy rights. While physical quartering of troops may seem an antiquated concern, questions about government intrusion into private spaces remain vital. Some scholars have suggested that the amendment's privacy protections might apply to modern contexts, such as government installation of surveillance equipment in private homes.

The Third Amendment stands as a reminder of how specific historical grievances can generate lasting constitutional principles. What began as a response to British colonial practices evolved into a fundamental protection of domestic privacy and civilian authority. While rarely invoked directly, its influence continues to shape American legal and political thought about the relationship between military power and individual rights.

The amendment's history also demonstrates how constitutional provisions can maintain relevance even as their original context fades. Though few Americans today fear literal quartering of troops, the amendment's underlying principles about privacy, civilian control, and limits on military power remain vital to constitutional democracy. In this way, the Third Amendment continues to contribute to the ongoing development of American constitutional law and civil liberties.

Search and Seizure: Fourth Amendment's Revolutionary Roots

The Fourth Amendment's origins lie deep in the colonial experience with British search and seizure practices, particularly the infamous writs of assistance that allowed customs officers virtually unlimited authority to search homes and businesses for smuggled goods. These general warrants became a flashpoint in the growing tension between colonial rights and British authority, setting the stage for what would become one of the most fundamental American constitutional protections.

The legal battle over general warrants began in earnest in 1761 when Boston attorney James Otis argued passionately against their renewal in a landmark court case. Though he lost the case, Otis's eloquent defense of privacy rights and his declaration that these writs placed "the liberty of every man in the hands of every petty officer" deeply influenced colonial thinking about search and seizure. John Adams, who witnessed the argument, later wrote that "then and there the child Independence was born."

British authorities relied heavily on general warrants to enforce increasingly unpopular trade regulations. Unlike specific warrants, which required detailed information about the place to be searched and items sought, general warrants gave officers broad discretion to search anywhere they suspected contraband might be found. This practice particularly affected merchants and ship owners in port cities, where customs officials regularly conducted invasive searches of homes, warehouses, and vessels.

The controversy wasn't limited to the colonies. In England, parallel legal battles were being fought over similar general warrants, particularly in the case of John Wilkes. Wilkes, a member of Parliament and publisher, successfully challenged the use of general warrants to search for seditious publications, establishing important common law precedents that would influence American law. The English courts' decisions in Wilkes's case and related matters helped establish the principle that searches required specific warrants based on probable cause.

As colonial resistance to British authority grew, the issue of unreasonable searches became increasingly intertwined with broader revolutionary sentiment. The Fourth Amendment's eventual text clearly reflected this experience: "The right of the people to be secure in their persons, houses, papers, and effects, against unreasonable searches and seizures, shall not be violated, and no Warrants shall issue, but upon probable cause, supported by Oath or affirmation, and particularly describing the place to be searched, and the persons or things to be seized."

The amendment's drafting during the Constitutional Convention and subsequent ratification debates revealed careful attention to balancing effective law enforcement with individual rights. The final language established both a broad protection against "unreasonable" searches and specific requirements for valid warrants. This dual structure would later prove crucial in constitutional interpretation, as courts grappled with what constituted "unreasonable" in various contexts.

Early American implementation of the Fourth Amendment focused primarily on physical searches of homes and businesses. The young republic's law enforcement needs were relatively simple, and the amendment's application straightforward. Courts generally required warrants for searches of private property, though various exceptions developed for emergencies and searches incident to arrest.

The Industrial Revolution and urbanization brought new challenges to Fourth Amendment interpretation. As cities grew and crime became more sophisticated, law enforcement agencies sought greater flexibility in conducting searches. Courts began developing more nuanced rules about what constituted reasonable searches in different contexts, while still maintaining the amendment's core protections against arbitrary government intrusion.

The advent of prohibition in the 1920s particularly tested Fourth Amendment principles. Federal agents conducting liquor raids often pushed the boundaries of permissible searches, leading to important Supreme Court decisions that helped define the amendment's scope. Cases from this era established the "exclusionary rule," which prohibited the use of illegally obtained evidence in court, giving the Fourth Amendment real enforcement teeth.

Technological advances repeatedly forced courts to reconsider Fourth Amendment applications. The invention of wiretapping raised questions about whether electronic surveillance constituted a "search" requiring a warrant. Initially, in Olmstead v. United States (1928), the Supreme Court held that wiretapping didn't implicate the Fourth Amendment because it involved no physical trespass. This narrow view would persist until 1967, when Katz v. United States established that the amendment protected people's reasonable expectations of privacy, not just physical spaces.

The automobile's widespread adoption created another challenge for Fourth Amendment doctrine. Cars' mobility made obtaining warrants impractical in many situations, leading courts to develop the "automobile exception" allowing warrantless searches based on probable cause. This practical accommodation demonstrated how Fourth Amendment principles could adapt to changing social conditions while maintaining their essential protective function.

The civil rights era brought renewed attention to search and seizure practices, particularly in urban communities where aggressive policing often led to constitutional violations. Cases from this period helped establish clearer standards for stop and frisk procedures, consent searches, and other common police practices. The Supreme Court's decisions sought to balance effective law enforcement with protection against racial discrimination and police harassment.

Modern Fourth Amendment jurisprudence continues to evolve with technological change. Digital devices, GPS tracking, thermal imaging, and other new technologies have forced courts to consider how colonial-era principles apply in a world the founders could never have imagined. Cases involving cell phone searches, computer data, and electronic surveillance have become increasingly common and complex.

The rise of terrorism concerns following the September 11 attacks created new tensions between security needs and Fourth Amendment rights. Government surveillance programs, particularly those involving bulk data collection, have raised novel constitutional questions about privacy in the digital age. Courts have generally tried to maintain traditional Fourth Amendment principles while acknowledging modern security challenges.

Today, the Fourth Amendment remains at the center of debates about privacy, technology, and security. Its fundamental principles about limiting government power and protecting individual privacy continue to shape law enforcement practices and individual rights. While the specific applications may have evolved far beyond what the founders envisioned, the amendment's core purpose of preventing arbitrary government intrusion into private life remains as relevant as ever.

Looking back at the Fourth Amendment's revolutionary roots reveals both continuity and change in American constitutional law. The colonial experience with general warrants created enduring principles about privacy and government power that continue to guide modern jurisprudence. Yet the amendment's application has proved remarkably adaptable, evolving to meet new challenges while maintaining its essential character as a bulwark against government overreach.

Justice for All: The Fifth Amendment's Protections

The Fifth Amendment stands as one of the most comprehensive protections of individual rights in the Constitution, emerging from centuries of struggle against arbitrary government power. Its five distinct guarantees, each addressing different aspects of legal justice, reflect hard-learned lessons from both English and colonial American history about the importance of protecting individuals facing state power.

The amendment's grand jury requirement grew from medieval English practice, where groups of citizens served as a buffer between accusers and accused. Colonial Americans had embraced grand juries not just as legal institutions but as political ones, using them to resist British authority by refusing to indict colonial protesters. This experience convinced the founders of the grand jury's importance as a check on government power.

Double jeopardy protections reflected ancient principles of English common law, codified in the maxim "nemo debet bis vexari pro una et eadem causa" (no one should be twice troubled for the same cause). The founders witnessed how British authorities sometimes tried colonists repeatedly for the same offense until achieving a conviction, leading them to enshrine this protection in the Constitution.

The right against self-incrimination, perhaps the amendment's most famous protection, emerged from resistance to the ecclesiastical courts' ex officio oath in England. These courts required defendants to swear to answer all questions truthfully before knowing the charges against them, effectively forcing self-incrimination. The practice was particularly abused in religious persecution cases, leading to its abolition in England and strong opposition in the colonies.

Colonial courts generally respected the right against self-incrimination, though its exact scope varied by jurisdiction. The constitutional protection went beyond colonial practice, establishing a broad right that would eventually be interpreted to cover any compelled testimony that might lead to criminal charges. This expansion reflected the founders' belief that forcing someone to testify against themselves was both morally wrong and practically unreliable.

The due process clause, stating that no person shall be deprived of "life, liberty, or property without due process of law," drew on Magna Carta's promise that no free man would be deprived of rights except "by the law of the land." This ancient protection against arbitrary government action had particular resonance for colonists who had experienced British violations of traditional legal rights.

Just compensation for government taking of private property completed the amendment's protections. This requirement grew from colonial experiences with British authorities seizing property without payment, particularly during the quartering of troops. The founders saw proper compensation as essential to protecting private property rights while allowing necessary government functions.

Early implementation of the Fifth Amendment focused primarily on federal criminal trials, as the Bill of Rights initially applied only to federal actions. States maintained their own varying levels of protection for these rights. The Supreme Court's early decisions generally interpreted the amendment's protections narrowly, though they recognized their fundamental importance to American justice.

The nineteenth century saw gradual expansion of Fifth Amendment protections through court decisions. The self-incrimination clause, in particular, gained broader interpretation, extending beyond criminal court testimony to cover any compelled statements that might lead to criminal prosecution. Courts also began developing more detailed standards for what constituted "due process" in various contexts.

The Civil War and Reconstruction brought new attention to due process rights, particularly as the Fourteenth Amendment made aspects of the Bill of Rights applicable to states. Though the Supreme Court initially resisted incorporating Fifth Amendment protections against state actions, gradually these fundamental rights were recognized as essential to American justice at all levels.

The Progressive Era brought new challenges to Fifth Amendment interpretation as government regulation of business increased. Cases involving economic regulations forced courts to consider what constituted proper compensation for government takings and what process was due when the state interfered with property rights. These decisions helped shape modern understanding of the amendment's scope.

The twentieth century saw dramatic expansion of Fifth Amendment protections, particularly regarding self-incrimination. The Supreme Court's decision in Miranda v. Arizona (1966) required police to inform suspects of their rights, including the right to remain silent, making the Fifth Amendment part of popular culture through "Miranda warnings." This decision reflected growing concern about protecting individual rights in the criminal justice system.

Modern Fifth Amendment jurisprudence continues to evolve with changing social conditions. Courts regularly face new questions about what constitutes self-incrimination in an age of digital evidence, when due process requires hearings versus other procedures, and what compensation is just when government regulations affect property values. These cases demonstrate the amendment's continuing vitality in protecting individual rights against government power.

The amendment's protections remain particularly relevant in an era of expanding government power and technological change. Questions about data privacy, regulatory takings, and procedural fairness in administrative proceedings all implicate Fifth Amendment rights. Courts continue to balance traditional protections with modern governmental needs, maintaining the amendment's core purpose while adapting to new circumstances.

Looking back at the Fifth Amendment's development reveals its essential role in American justice. From its origins in ancient English law through its modern applications, it has provided fundamental protections for individuals facing state power. While its interpretation has evolved, its basic principles about fairness, dignity, and protection against government overreach remain as vital today as when first adopted.

Fair Trials: The Sixth Amendment Revolution

The right to a fair trial stands as one of the most fundamental guarantees in American law, and the Sixth Amendment codified this essential protection in unprecedented detail. Born from bitter colonial experiences with British judicial abuses, the amendment established comprehensive standards for criminal trials that continue to shape American justice today.

Colonial Americans had witnessed firsthand how an unfair judicial system could become a tool of oppression. British authorities routinely denied accused colonists basic procedural rights, trying them in admiralty courts without juries, delaying trials indefinitely, and preventing access to witnesses and evidence. These experiences made the founders keenly aware of the need for explicit trial protections in the new Constitution.

The amendment begins with the right to a speedy trial, addressing the common British practice of leaving accused colonists to languish in jail for extended periods awaiting their day in court. This delay served as both punishment and pressure to plead guilty, a tactic the founders sought to prevent. They understood that justice delayed often meant justice denied, particularly for those who couldn't afford bail.

The requirement for a public trial reflected long-standing English common law tradition, but took on new importance in America. Secret trials had been used for political persecution in England, and the founders believed public scrutiny was essential to ensuring fair proceedings. This transparency requirement became a cornerstone of American judicial practice, though courts would later recognize limited exceptions for national security and privacy concerns.

Perhaps most importantly, the amendment guaranteed trial by an impartial jury. While jury trials existed in colonial America, British authorities had increasingly bypassed them in favor of admiralty courts or military tribunals. The founders saw juries as essential protections against government overreach, placing citizens as buffers between prosecutors and the accused. This right would later be interpreted to require juries drawn from a cross-section of the community, though achieving truly representative juries remained a challenge through much of American history.

The amendment also guaranteed defendants the right to be informed of charges against them and to confront their accusers. These provisions addressed the British practice of holding trials based on secret evidence or anonymous accusations. The confrontation clause, in particular, established the principle that evidence against a defendant must be presented in open court where it can be challenged through cross-examination.

The right to compulsory process for obtaining witnesses ensured defendants could present their full defense. Under British rule, accused colonists often struggled to compel testimony from witnesses in their favor, particularly government officials. This provision leveled the playing field, giving defendants the same power as prosecutors to require witness testimony.

The right to counsel completed the amendment's protections, though its initial scope was limited. In colonial times, defendants in serious criminal cases often faced prosecution without lawyers, as British practice generally denied counsel except in minor cases. The amendment guaranteed the right to retain counsel, but it would take nearly two centuries before this evolved into a requirement that the government provide lawyers for defendants who couldn't afford them.

Early implementation of these rights varied significantly by jurisdiction. Federal courts generally enforced them strictly, but state courts, not yet bound by the Bill of Rights, maintained varying standards. Some states provided broader protections than the federal government, while others offered fewer safeguards. This patchwork of protections would persist until the twentieth century.

The Civil War era brought new challenges to fair trial rights, particularly in the military justice system. The Supreme Court's ex parte Milligan decision (1866) reaffirmed civilians' right to jury trial even during wartime, though military necessity would remain a recurring exception to Sixth Amendment protections.

The twentieth century saw dramatic expansion of trial rights through Supreme Court decisions incorporating the Sixth Amendment against the states via the Fourteenth Amendment. Cases like Gideon v. Wainwright (1963) established the right to appointed counsel for indigent defendants, while others set standards for jury selection, speedy trial requirements, and confrontation rights.

Modern interpretation of Sixth Amendment rights continues to evolve with changing circumstances. Courts regularly face new questions about how traditional protections apply to contemporary challenges: When does the right to counsel begin in complex investigations? How should confrontation rights apply to digital evidence or child witnesses? What constitutes a speedy trial in an overloaded justice system?

Technology has created particular challenges for Sixth Amendment rights. Video conferencing, digital evidence, and social media have transformed both the nature of criminal evidence and trial procedures. Courts struggle to balance traditional confrontation rights with new forms of testimony and evidence, while ensuring trials remain both efficient and fair.

The right to counsel has become increasingly critical as criminal law grows more complex. Modern defendants face intricate procedures, complex evidence, and severe consequences that make legal representation essential for a fair trial. Yet public defender systems often lack resources to provide effective assistance, raising questions about whether the amendment's promises are being fully met.

Looking ahead, the Sixth Amendment's guarantees face continuing challenges from terrorism, technology, and systemic pressures on the criminal justice system. Yet its core principle remains vital: ensuring fair trials through specific, enforceable procedural protections. The amendment's detailed requirements continue to guide courts in balancing efficiency with fairness, security with transparency, and government power with individual rights.

Civil Justice: Seventh Amendment's Forgotten Importance

The Seventh Amendment's guarantee of civil jury trials stands as one of the Constitution's most overlooked yet historically significant protections. While modern discussions of constitutional rights often focus on criminal proceedings, the founders considered civil jury trials equally essential to protecting liberty and property from government overreach.

Colonial Americans had learned to cherish civil juries as bulwarks against British authority. Royal governors and judges frequently attempted to bypass local juries in civil cases, especially in customs disputes where colonial merchants faced penalties for violating British trade regulations. Juries often refused to enforce these unpopular laws, leading British authorities to expand the jurisdiction of juryless admiralty courts. This erosion of jury rights became a major grievance leading to the Revolution.

The original Constitution's failure to explicitly protect civil jury trials sparked significant opposition during ratification debates. Anti-Federalists argued that without such protection, the new federal government could gradually eliminate jury trials in civil cases, just as the British had attempted. This concern resonated deeply with citizens who viewed civil juries as essential safeguards of their rights against powerful interests.

The Seventh Amendment addressed these fears by preserving jury trials in civil cases while acknowledging practical limitations. Its language, preserving the right to jury trial "in suits at common law" where the amount in controversy exceeds twenty dollars, reflected careful compromise. The reference to common law distinguished cases traditionally decided by juries from those handled by courts of equity, where juries were historically not used.

This distinction between law and equity, though archaic to modern ears, shaped the amendment's application throughout American history. Courts have generally interpreted it to preserve jury trials in cases seeking monetary damages, while allowing judges alone to handle cases seeking injunctions or other equitable remedies. This framework has proven remarkably adaptable to changing legal circumstances.

The amendment's twenty-dollar threshold, though seemingly trivial today, represented a meaningful sum in 1791. The founders set it low to ensure broad access to juries while preventing trivial cases from overwhelming courts. While inflation has rendered this figure largely meaningless, courts have maintained it as written, though practical considerations and court rules now impose higher thresholds for federal cases.

Perhaps the amendment's most significant feature is its second clause, which limits courts' ability to overturn jury verdicts. By specifying that "no fact tried by a jury, shall be otherwise re-examined in any Court of the United States," the amendment protected jury decisions from casual reversal by judges. This provision reflected deep distrust of judicial power and determination to preserve juries' role in deciding factual disputes.

Early implementation of the Seventh Amendment revealed its complexity. Federal courts developed detailed rules about when jury trials were required, drawing on historical practice and practical necessity. State courts, not bound by the amendment until modern times, developed varying approaches to civil juries, though most state constitutions contained similar protections.

The nineteenth century saw civil juries play crucial roles in resolving disputes during America's rapid expansion. Juries decided countless cases involving property rights, business contracts, and personal injuries. Their decisions helped shape common law development and often reflected community values in ways that formal legal rules could not capture.

The rise of administrative agencies in the twentieth century presented new challenges to civil jury rights. As government regulation expanded, agencies increasingly adjudicated disputes through administrative proceedings without juries. Courts generally allowed this practice for "public rights" cases involving government benefits or regulatory enforcement, while preserving jury trials for traditional private rights disputes.

Modern civil litigation has raised new questions about the amendment's scope. Complex technical evidence, class actions, and multidistrict litigation strain traditional jury trial procedures. Courts struggle to balance the right to jury trial with needs for efficiency and expertise in managing complicated cases.

The growth of alternative dispute resolution has also affected civil jury rights. Arbitration agreements increasingly route disputes away from courts entirely, raising concerns about erosion of jury trial rights. While courts generally enforce such agreements, debate continues about their impact on constitutional protections.

Cost and delay in civil litigation present practical challenges to jury trial rights. Extended proceedings and expensive legal representation make jury trials prohibitively expensive for many litigants. This reality often forces settlement of cases that historically would have reached juries, effectively limiting the amendment's practical impact.

Despite these challenges, civil juries continue to serve important functions in American law. They provide community input on important disputes, check judicial and governmental power, and ensure public participation in civil justice. Their decisions in cases involving civil rights, consumer protection, and corporate responsibility often reflect evolving social values and influence legal development.

Looking ahead, the Seventh Amendment's protections face continuing pressure from forces seeking to streamline civil justice through non-jury procedures. Yet its core guarantee remains vital to American democracy, ensuring that citizens maintain direct involvement in resolving civil disputes. While its application may evolve with changing circumstances, the amendment's fundamental promise of civil jury trials endures as an important safeguard of liberty and justice.

Cruel and Unusual: Eighth Amendment Debates

The Eighth Amendment's prohibition of cruel and unusual punishment emerged from centuries of struggle against brutal state sanctioned violence. While its twenty-three words may seem straightforward, the amendment's interpretation has sparked intense debates throughout American history about the limits of state power and the meaning of human dignity.

The amendment's roots trace back to the English Bill of Rights of 1689, which sought to curb the excesses of Stuart monarchs who had employed horrific punishments against political opponents. Colonial Americans, familiar with British penal practices, incorporated similar protections into several state constitutions before the federal Bill of Rights. The founders viewed excessive punishment not just as humanitarian concern but as a tool of tyranny that could be used to suppress political dissent.

During ratification debates, Anti-Federalists argued forcefully for explicit restrictions on federal punishment powers. They feared that without such limits, the new government might employ harsh British-style punishments like drawing and quartering, burning at the stake, or extended torture. The Eighth Amendment addressed these concerns by adopting language similar to existing state provisions, though debate persisted about its precise scope.

Early interpretations focused primarily on prohibiting obviously cruel methods of punishment rather than questioning the proportionality of sentences. Courts generally deferred to legislative judgments about appropriate penalties, intervening only in cases of clearly barbaric practices. This approach reflected the amendment's origins as a ban on torture and deliberately cruel methods rather than a broader mandate to regulate punishment.

The nineteenth century saw gradual evolution in punishment practices, with many states moving away from public corporal punishment toward imprisonment. However, conditions in many prisons were horrific, raising questions about whether prolonged incarceration in deplorable conditions violated the amendment. Courts struggled to define when poor prison conditions crossed the constitutional line.

A major shift began in the 1950s and 1960s as courts increasingly examined whether punishments were proportional to crimes. The Supreme Court developed tests considering whether penalties were grossly disproportionate or shocked the conscience of civilized society. This approach opened new avenues for challenging not just methods of punishment but also sentence lengths and conditions of confinement.

The death penalty has generated the most sustained Eighth Amendment controversy. In 1972, the Supreme Court temporarily halted all executions, finding that arbitrary and discriminatory application of capital punishment violated the amendment. States responded by revising death penalty laws to provide more structured procedures, leading the Court to accept reformed capital punishment systems in 1976.

Subsequent death penalty challenges have focused on particular applications, leading to prohibitions on executing mentally disabled offenders, juvenile offenders, and those convicted of non-homicide crimes. Courts have also scrutinized execution methods, requiring states to avoid unnecessary pain while acknowledging that some discomfort may be inevitable in carrying out capital sentences.

Prison conditions have become another major focus of Eighth Amendment litigation. Courts have held that deliberate indifference to serious medical needs, failure to protect inmates from violence, and severely inadequate living conditions can constitute cruel and unusual punishment. These decisions have forced significant reforms in many prison systems while generating ongoing debate about minimum constitutional standards.

The amendment's application to juvenile offenders has evolved significantly. Courts have increasingly recognized that children's reduced culpability and capacity for rehabilitation require different constitutional standards. This has led to restrictions on juvenile life sentences without parole and greater emphasis on rehabilitation rather than punishment for young offenders.

Modern Eighth Amendment jurisprudence increasingly considers evolving standards of decency, looking to contemporary values rather than eighteenth-century standards. This approach has allowed the amendment's meaning to develop with changing social norms while generating criticism from those who prefer more fixed historical interpretation.

Scientific evidence has influenced recent Eighth Amendment analysis, particularly regarding mental illness, addiction, and brain development. Courts have considered research on pain perception in evaluating execution methods and psychological evidence in assessing the impact of solitary confinement. This integration of scientific knowledge with constitutional analysis continues to shape the amendment's application.

International comparisons have also informed modern interpretation, though their role remains controversial. Advocates argue that widespread international rejection of practices like capital punishment or juvenile life sentences indicates evolving standards of decency. Critics contend that American constitutional interpretation should not be influenced by foreign practices.

The opioid crisis and mass incarceration have raised new Eighth Amendment questions about treating addiction as a crime and imposing lengthy sentences for non-violent drug offenses. Some argue that current drug policies constitute cruel and unusual punishment given modern understanding of addiction as a medical condition rather than moral failing.

Looking ahead, emerging technologies like chemical restraints, surveillance systems, and automated confinement may present novel Eighth Amendment issues. Courts will need to evaluate whether new control methods, though perhaps less physically brutal than historical punishments, might nevertheless constitute cruel and unusual punishment through psychological impact or dignity violation.

Climate change has introduced additional concerns as rising temperatures make many prisons dangerously hot and natural disasters threaten inmate safety. Courts increasingly face questions about whether housing prisoners in facilities without adequate climate control or evacuation plans violates the Eighth Amendment.

The amendment's future interpretation will likely continue balancing historical understanding with evolving standards of decency. As society's understanding of punishment, rehabilitation, and human dignity develops, the Eighth Amendment remains a crucial check on government power to punish, adapting to new challenges while preserving its core purpose of preventing state cruelty.

Hidden Rights: The Ninth Amendment Mystery

The Ninth Amendment remains one of the Constitution's most enigmatic provisions, stating simply that the enumeration of certain rights shall not be construed to deny or disparage others retained by the people. This seemingly straightforward declaration has sparked centuries of debate about its meaning and implications for American liberty.

The amendment emerged from heated debates during the Constitution's ratification. Many Anti-Federalists worried that listing specific rights in the Bill of Rights might imply that unlisted rights had no protection. James Madison, responding to these concerns, crafted the Ninth Amendment as a safeguard against the notion that enumerated rights were the only ones citizens possessed.

Early American legal theory recognized numerous natural rights beyond those explicitly mentioned in the Constitution. These included personal autonomy, self-defense, and the pursuit of livelihood. The Ninth Amendment aimed to preserve these traditional common law and natural rights from government encroachment, though its practical effect remained largely theoretical for many decades.

Throughout the nineteenth century, courts rarely invoked the Ninth Amendment directly. Instead, judges typically relied on other constitutional provisions or common law principles when protecting individual rights. This judicial reluctance reflected uncertainty about how to identify and enforce unenumerated rights without clear textual guidance.

The amendment gained renewed attention during the twentieth century's rights revolution. Justice Arthur Goldberg's influential concurrence in Griswold v. Connecticut cited the Ninth Amendment as support for constitutional privacy rights. This sparked fresh scholarly interest in the amendment's potential as a source of previously unrecognized constitutional protections.

Critics argued that the Ninth Amendment was merely a rule of construction, intended to prevent a particular misreading of the Bill of Rights rather than create substantive rights. They warned that using the amendment to recognize new rights would give judges too much discretion and undermine democratic governance.

Supporters countered that the amendment's text and history clearly contemplate substantive protection for unenumerated rights. They argued that ignoring such rights would betray the founders' vision of limited government and broad individual liberty. This debate continues to influence constitutional interpretation today.

The amendment's modern significance extends beyond traditional legal disputes. Environmental advocates have suggested it might protect rights to clean air and water. Privacy advocates cite it in debates about digital surveillance and data protection. Some argue it supports educational rights or healthcare access.

The rise of originalist legal theory has complicated Ninth Amendment interpretation. Originalists struggle to reconcile the amendment's open-ended language with their preference for fixed constitutional meaning. Some propose focusing on rights recognized in 1791, while others acknowledge the need for evolution in identifying protected rights.

State constitutions often provide explicit protection for rights merely implied by the federal Ninth Amendment. This state-level recognition has sometimes influenced federal constitutional interpretation, suggesting how unenumerated rights might be identified and protected.

The amendment's relationship with the Fourteenth Amendment remains contested. Some scholars argue that the Fourteenth Amendment's privileges or immunities clause incorporates Ninth Amendment rights against state governments. Others maintain that the Ninth Amendment simply limits federal power without affecting state authority.

Modern technology has raised new questions about the amendment's scope. As digital innovation creates novel privacy concerns and forms of personal expression, courts increasingly face questions about whether traditional rights frameworks adequately protect modern liberty interests.

The amendment's role in protecting economic liberty remains particularly controversial. While some argue it preserves economic rights like occupational freedom and contract rights, others contend that post-New Deal jurisprudence properly limits economic due process claims.

International human rights law has influenced some scholars' understanding of the Ninth Amendment. They suggest that widely recognized human rights might inform the identification of unenumerated constitutional rights, though this approach remains controversial.

The amendment's implications for emerging rights claims continue to evolve. Advocates have invoked it in debates about reproductive rights, sexual orientation, gender identity, and personal autonomy. These controversies highlight the ongoing challenge of balancing individual liberty with democratic governance.

Looking forward, the Ninth Amendment seems likely to play an increasingly important role in constitutional discourse. As society faces new challenges involving technology, privacy, and personal autonomy, this mysterious provision may finally emerge from the shadows to help define the boundaries of American liberty.

The amendment's true significance may lie not in any particular application but in its reminder that constitutional rights transcend explicit text. It stands as a perpetual challenge to legal formalism and an invitation to consider the full scope of human freedom in a democratic society.

State Power: Tenth Amendment's Federal Balance

The Tenth Amendment established one of the Constitution's most fundamental principles: that powers not delegated to the federal government are reserved to the states or to the people. This deceptively simple statement has profoundly shaped American federalism, sparking centuries of debate about the proper balance between state and federal authority.

The amendment emerged from intense ratification debates where Anti-Federalists feared an all-powerful central government would overwhelm state sovereignty. James Madison and other Federalists initially argued that such an amendment was unnecessary, since the Constitution already created a government of limited, enumerated powers. However, they ultimately supported it to secure ratification and reassure skeptics that states would retain significant authority.

Early Supreme Court decisions generally interpreted the Tenth Amendment as a robust constraint on federal power. Chief Justice John Marshall, while establishing broad federal authority in cases like McCulloch v. Maryland, nevertheless acknowledged that the amendment preserved meaningful state sovereignty. States maintained primary responsibility for criminal law, property rights, education, and most aspects of daily governance.

The Civil War fundamentally altered this balance. The Thirteenth, Fourteenth, and Fifteenth Amendments dramatically expanded federal authority to protect individual rights against state infringement. This shift challenged traditional understandings of state sovereignty, though the Tenth Amendment remained an important principle of constitutional structure.

The Progressive Era brought new tensions as expanding federal regulation encountered Tenth Amendment objections. Early twentieth century courts sometimes invoked the amendment to strike down federal laws addressing child labor, manufacturing conditions, and other social issues. This doctrinal approach reached its apex during the New Deal, when the Supreme Court initially rejected several Roosevelt administration programs on federalism grounds.

However, the Court's famous "switch in time" of 1937 marked a retreat from strict Tenth Amendment limits on federal power. For several decades afterward, the amendment was widely viewed as a mere "truism" with little practical effect. Congress passed sweeping legislation addressing civil rights, environmental protection, workplace safety, and numerous other areas previously considered state domains.

The 1976 case National League of Cities v. Usery briefly revived the Tenth Amendment as a constraint on federal authority, holding that Congress couldn't regulate state employees' wages and hours. This decision suggested the amendment protected core state functions from federal interference. However, the Court overruled this precedent less than a decade later, returning to a more limited view of Tenth Amendment constraints.

Modern Tenth Amendment doctrine has evolved into a nuanced framework balancing state and federal interests. While Congress maintains broad regulatory authority under the Commerce Clause and Spending Clause, the Court has identified certain limits. Federal laws cannot "commandeer" state officials to implement federal programs or coerce states through excessively conditional funding.

Environmental regulation has become a major Tenth Amendment battleground. States challenge federal environmental rules as intrusive, while defenders argue that pollution and climate change require national solutions. Similar debates arise over education policy, healthcare regulation, and numerous other areas where state and federal authority overlap.

The amendment has gained renewed prominence in debates over marijuana legalization, sanctuary cities, and other instances of state resistance to federal policy. Some scholars argue these conflicts reflect the amendment's core purpose of enabling states to serve as laboratories of democracy and checks on federal power.

Conservative legal theorists often invoke the Tenth Amendment to challenge federal regulatory authority, while progressives typically favor broader federal power to address national problems. This ideological division reflects deeper disagreements about government's proper role and the meaning of American federalism.

The growth of cooperative federalism, where federal and state governments share regulatory responsibility, has complicated traditional Tenth Amendment analysis. Modern governance often involves complex partnerships that blur clear jurisdictional lines. Courts struggle to apply eighteenth century federalism principles to these collaborative arrangements.

State constitutions and legislation increasingly assert Tenth Amendment principles, sometimes claiming authority to nullify federal laws deemed unconstitutional. While courts generally reject such extreme positions, these efforts highlight ongoing tensions in American federalism.

The amendment's relationship with individual rights remains contested. Some argue it protects personal liberty by limiting federal power, while others contend strong federal authority is necessary to secure constitutional rights. This debate reflects the challenge of balancing local autonomy with national standards.

Looking ahead, the Tenth Amendment seems likely to remain central to American constitutional discourse. As society faces new challenges requiring coordinated responses, questions of federal versus state authority will continue to shape policy debates. The amendment's enduring significance lies in its role structuring these essential conversations about American governance.

The rise of global challenges like climate change, pandemics, and economic integration may further test traditional notions of state sovereignty. Yet the Tenth Amendment's basic principle that power should be divided and restrained remains vital to American democracy. It continues to inform how we balance local autonomy with national needs in an increasingly interconnected world.

Presidential Succession: The Eleventh Amendment Crisis

The Eleventh Amendment emerged from a constitutional crisis that threatened the young nation's stability, centering on fundamental questions about state sovereignty and federal court power. The controversy began with the 1793 Supreme Court case Chisholm v. Georgia, where a South Carolina citizen sued Georgia to recover debts from the Revolutionary War. Georgia refused to appear in court, claiming sovereign immunity protected states from being sued by citizens of other states in federal court.

The Supreme Court, led by Chief Justice John Jay, ruled against Georgia, interpreting Article III of the Constitution to allow such suits. This decision sent shockwaves through the states, which feared being overwhelmed by private debt claims in federal courts. Many states faced significant Revolutionary War debts and worried that federal courts would force them to pay creditors, potentially bankrupting state treasuries.

The reaction was swift and nearly unanimous. Within two days of the Chisholm decision, members of Congress proposed what would become the Eleventh Amendment. The states ratified it with unprecedented speed, making it the first constitutional amendment adopted after the Bill of Rights. The amendment's text explicitly prohibited federal courts from hearing suits against states by citizens of other states or foreign nations.

However, the amendment's apparently straightforward language has generated complex interpretations and debates. Early Supreme Court decisions expanded its reach beyond the literal text. In Hans v. Louisiana (1890), the Court held that the amendment's principle of state sovereign immunity also prevented citizens from suing their own states in federal court, despite this scenario not being explicitly mentioned in the amendment's text.

This broad interpretation reflected deeper constitutional tensions about federalism and state sovereignty. The Court viewed the Eleventh Amendment as confirming a fundamental principle of state sovereign immunity that predated the Constitution itself. This understanding transformed the amendment from a narrow procedural rule into a broader statement about state-federal relations.

The amendment's impact on American governance has been profound and sometimes controversial. It has shielded states from numerous lawsuits seeking monetary damages, affecting areas from state employment to environmental regulation. States can still be sued in their own courts if they consent, and Congress can sometimes abrogate state immunity when enforcing other constitutional provisions, particularly the Fourteenth Amendment.

Modern Eleventh Amendment jurisprudence has evolved into a complex framework balancing state sovereignty with the need for accountability. The Supreme Court has recognized several important exceptions to state immunity. Federal courts can hear suits against state officials seeking injunctive relief to stop ongoing constitutional violations, known as the Ex parte Young doctrine. This exception ensures states cannot simply ignore federal law while hiding behind sovereign immunity.

The amendment has particularly significant implications for civil rights enforcement. While individuals cannot directly sue states for monetary damages under many federal laws, they can often sue state officials for prospective relief or pursue claims through state courts. This framework attempts to balance respect for state sovereignty with the necessity of ensuring state compliance with federal law.

Business interests and creditors have long sought ways around Eleventh Amendment immunity, leading to creative legal strategies and statutory schemes. Congress has sometimes conditioned federal funding on state waiver of immunity, creating indirect pressure for states to accept certain types of suits. These arrangements demonstrate how modern governance has adapted to work within the amendment's constraints.

Environmental regulation provides a telling example of these dynamics. While states generally cannot be sued directly for damages under federal environmental laws, the Environmental Protection Agency and private parties can seek injunctive relief to stop ongoing violations. This system has evolved to enable environmental protection while respecting state sovereign immunity.

The amendment continues to generate significant litigation and academic debate. Some scholars argue its interpretation has strayed too far from its original purpose of preventing specific types of diversity jurisdiction suits. Others contend the Court's broad reading appropriately protects essential principles of state sovereignty in our federal system.

Recent Supreme Court decisions have generally maintained robust state immunity while refining its contours. Questions persist about how the doctrine applies to new situations, such as suits involving state-affiliated entities or novel statutory schemes. The Court continues to balance competing principles of state sovereignty, federal supremacy, and individual rights.

The Eleventh Amendment's legacy extends beyond its specific legal effects. It represents an early example of how constitutional crisis can lead to formal amendment, demonstrating the Constitution's adaptability. It also illustrates how constitutional provisions can evolve through judicial interpretation to address changing circumstances while maintaining core principles.

Looking ahead, the amendment's importance seems likely to grow as states face new challenges requiring careful balance of state and federal authority. From cybersecurity to public health emergencies, questions of state immunity and federal court jurisdiction remain vital to American governance. The Eleventh Amendment's principles continue to shape how these issues are resolved, demonstrating the enduring relevance of this early constitutional adjustment.

Electoral Reform: Twelfth Amendment Changes

The Twelfth Amendment emerged from the chaotic presidential election of 1800, which exposed serious flaws in the Constitution's original system for selecting presidents and vice presidents. Under the initial design, each elector cast two votes for president, with the runner up becoming vice president. This arrangement, while appearing elegant in theory, proved disastrous in practice as political parties emerged and electors sought to coordinate their votes strategically.

The crisis came to a head in 1800 when Democratic-Republican electors, attempting to elect both Thomas Jefferson as president and Aaron Burr as vice president, failed to differentiate their votes between the two positions. The result was a tie between Jefferson and Burr, throwing the election into the House of Representatives. The ensuing deadlock lasted through 36 ballots over seven days, nearly creating a constitutional crisis as the nation approached Inauguration Day without a clear successor to President John Adams.

The resolution finally came when Alexander Hamilton, despite his personal antipathy toward Jefferson, helped persuade several Federalist representatives to abstain, allowing Jefferson's election. However, the experience convinced political leaders that the electoral system needed immediate reform to prevent similar crises in the future. The Twelfth Amendment, ratified in 1804, fundamentally altered the Electoral College by requiring electors to cast separate ballots for president and vice president.

This change might seem technical, but it represented a significant shift in American political development. By acknowledging the reality of partisan tickets, the amendment effectively legitimized the role of political parties in presidential elections. No longer would the president and vice president potentially come from opposing parties, as had happened in 1796 when Federalist John Adams served with his Democratic-Republican rival Jefferson.

The amendment also modified the contingent election procedure used when no candidate receives an electoral majority. Under the new system, if no presidential candidate wins a majority, the House chooses from the top three candidates rather than five, with each state delegation casting a single vote. For vice presidential deadlocks, the Senate selects between the top two candidates. These changes streamlined the process while maintaining the federal character of the contingent election system.

Critics at the time worried that the amendment would diminish the vice presidency by making it subordinate to the presidency. Some feared that parties would nominate inferior candidates for the second position, knowing they would no longer accidentally become president. These concerns proved somewhat prescient, as the vice presidency indeed became a less independently powerful office, though it would later evolve into a more significant role through other means.

The amendment's impact extended beyond its immediate electoral reforms. By formally recognizing the two-person ticket, it helped shape the development of American campaign practices. Parties began more carefully considering regional and ideological balance in their tickets, leading to the familiar pattern of choosing running mates to complement the presidential nominee's perceived weaknesses or expand their electoral appeal.

Implementation of the new system proceeded smoothly in subsequent elections, demonstrating the amendment's success in addressing the specific problems that had prompted its adoption. The 1804 election, the first conducted under the new rules, saw Jefferson and his chosen running mate George Clinton win decisively without any of the complications that had plagued the previous contest.

The Twelfth Amendment's provisions have largely withstood the test of time, though some aspects have generated controversy in modern elections. The winner-take-all allocation of electoral votes adopted by most states, while not mandated by the amendment, has become a focus of reform efforts. Similarly, questions about faithless electors and the role of the Electoral College itself continue to spark debate.

The amendment's legacy includes several near-invocations of its contingent election procedures. The 1824 election saw Andrew Jackson win a plurality of both popular and electoral votes but lose in the House to John Quincy Adams. In 1876, disputed electoral votes nearly triggered another contingent election before the Compromise of 1877 resolved the situation. These episodes demonstrate both the amendment's importance as a constitutional safety valve and the continuing challenges of presidential selection.

Modern scholars often point to the Twelfth Amendment as an example of successful constitutional adaptation to political reality. Rather than maintaining a system based on theoretical ideals about nonpartisan selection of national leaders, the amendment pragmatically accommodated the emergence of organized political parties. This flexibility helped stabilize American democracy during its crucial early period.

The amendment also illustrates how constitutional changes can have unintended consequences that reshape political institutions over time. While focused on solving specific electoral problems, it contributed to the development of the modern two-party system and influenced how Americans think about presidential tickets and campaigns. These broader effects remind us that constitutional amendments often work in subtle ways to shape political development.

Today, as debates about electoral reform continue, the Twelfth Amendment's history offers important lessons about adapting constitutional structures to changing political circumstances. Whether considering proposals for direct popular election or other modifications to the Electoral College, understanding how and why the Twelfth Amendment transformed the original system remains relevant to contemporary discussions about presidential selection.

The Great Emancipation: Thirteenth Amendment's Journey

The abolition of slavery stands as perhaps the most transformative change ever made to the United States Constitution, emerging from the nation's bloodiest conflict and fundamentally reshaping American society. The Thirteenth Amendment's journey from radical proposition to constitutional law reflects both the immense struggle required to end America's "peculiar institution" and the revolutionary impact of this change on the nation's legal and social fabric.

The path to the Thirteenth Amendment began long before the Civil War, in the persistent efforts of abolitionists who spent decades fighting against slavery through moral suasion, political action, and direct resistance. Frederick Douglass, William Lloyd Garrison, Sojourner Truth, and countless others laid the groundwork by forcing the nation to confront slavery's fundamental contradiction with American ideals of freedom and equality.

By 1860, the political battle over slavery's expansion had fractured the nation. Abraham Lincoln's election, though he campaigned primarily on preventing slavery's spread rather than immediate abolition, triggered Southern secession and civil war. The conflict's early years saw a gradual evolution in Northern war aims, from preservation of the Union alone to emancipation as a military necessity and finally to universal abolition as a moral imperative.

The amendment's actual drafting began in 1864, with several versions considered before the final language emerged: "Neither slavery nor involuntary servitude, except as a punishment for crime whereof the party shall have been duly convicted, shall exist within the United States, or any place subject to their jurisdiction." This deceptively simple sentence represented a revolutionary change, directly overturning the Constitution's previous accommodation of slavery and establishing federal power to protect individual freedom.

The congressional debate over the amendment revealed the profound transformation in American political thought wrought by the Civil War. Representatives who just years earlier had pledged never to interfere with Southern slavery now argued passionately for universal emancipation. The amendment passed the Senate in April 1864 but initially failed in the House, leading Lincoln to personally lobby members and make ratification a central issue of his 1864 reelection campaign.

The House finally passed the amendment in January 1865, setting off jubilant celebrations among abolitionists and their allies. The ratification process that followed highlighted the complex political dynamics of Reconstruction. Southern states were required to ratify the Thirteenth Amendment as a condition of readmission to the Union, creating an unusual situation where defeated Confederate states helped pass the very reform they had gone to war to prevent.

The amendment's impact extended far beyond the formal abolition of chattel slavery. Its second section, granting Congress power to enforce the ban on slavery through appropriate legislation, became the basis for numerous civil rights laws aimed at securing genuine freedom for former slaves. This enforcement power represented a significant expansion of federal authority to protect individual rights, setting important precedents for later constitutional developments.

The amendment's reference to "involuntary servitude" proved particularly significant, as courts interpreted this phrase to prohibit various forms of coerced labor beyond traditional slavery. This broader reading allowed the amendment to address peonage, debt bondage, and other systems of labor exploitation that emerged in slavery's aftermath. However, the "punishment for crime" exception created a troubling loophole that Southern states exploited through convict lease systems and other discriminatory practices.

Implementation of the Thirteenth Amendment faced immediate challenges. While it effectively ended legal slavery, securing genuine freedom for former slaves required additional constitutional reforms, particularly the Fourteenth and Fifteenth Amendments. The rise of Black Codes, sharecropping, and other restrictive practices demonstrated how former slave states sought to maintain systems of racial control even after formal emancipation.

The Supreme Court's early interpretations of the amendment reflected these tensions. In the Civil Rights Cases of 1883, the Court narrowly construed Congress's enforcement power, ruling that the amendment prohibited only actual slavery and involuntary servitude rather than broader forms of racial discrimination. This restrictive reading limited the amendment's effectiveness as a tool for achieving full racial equality.

Nevertheless, the Thirteenth Amendment's fundamental transformation of American society cannot be overstated. It eliminated the constitutional protection of human property, established the principle of universal freedom under federal law, and created new congressional power to protect individual rights. These changes laid the groundwork for the modern civil rights movement and continuing efforts to achieve racial justice.

The amendment's legacy continues to evolve. Modern courts have recognized its relevance to contemporary forms of exploitation, including human trafficking and forced labor. Legal scholars have argued for broader interpretations that would address persistent racial inequalities rooted in slavery's aftermath. These ongoing debates demonstrate how the Thirteenth Amendment remains a living force in American law and society.

The ratification of the Thirteenth Amendment marked a decisive break with America's slave-holding past and established new constitutional principles of freedom and federal protection of individual rights. While its promise of genuine liberation remained incomplete, its fundamental reshaping of American law and society made possible the continuing struggle for racial justice and human dignity.

Liberty and Citizenship: Early Days of the Fourteenth

The Fourteenth Amendment's early years represent one of the most turbulent and consequential periods in American constitutional history, as the nation grappled with the monumental task of defining citizenship and civil rights in the aftermath of slavery. The amendment's adoption in 1868 marked the beginning rather than the end of a profound struggle over the meaning of American freedom and equality.

The immediate context for the Fourteenth Amendment was the resistance of former Confederate states to extending basic rights to freed slaves. Despite the Thirteenth Amendment's abolition of slavery, Southern states enacted Black Codes that severely restricted African Americans' freedom of movement, right to own property, and ability to enter contracts. These laws threatened to create a new form of quasi-slavery, prompting Congress to seek stronger constitutional protections for civil rights.

Representative John Bingham of Ohio emerged as the primary architect of the amendment's crucial first section, which established both national citizenship and fundamental rights protections. The citizenship clause directly overturned the Supreme Court's infamous Dred Scott decision, declaring that "all persons born or naturalized in the United States" were citizens of both the nation and their state of residence. This revolutionary provision established citizenship as a national right rather than a state-determined status.

The amendment's due process and equal protection clauses introduced equally radical changes, prohibiting states from abridging the "privileges or immunities" of citizens, depriving any person of "life, liberty, or property without due process of law," or denying "equal protection of the laws." These sweeping guarantees represented the first constitutional limitations on state power to violate individual rights, fundamentally altering the federal system.

Congressional debates over the amendment revealed both its transformative aspirations and its political limitations. Radical Republicans sought comprehensive protection for civil rights, while moderates focused more narrowly on preventing the worst abuses of state power. The final text reflected this tension, establishing broad principles while leaving their specific application to future interpretation.

Initial enforcement of the Fourteenth Amendment occurred through a series of Reconstruction-era civil rights laws. The Civil Rights Act of 1866, which Congress reenacted after the amendment's ratification, guaranteed equal rights in property ownership, contract formation, and court access. The Enforcement Act of 1870 provided federal protection for voting rights, while the Civil Rights Act of 1875 prohibited discrimination in public accommodations.

However, the amendment's early promise faced immediate challenges. White supremacist violence, including widespread attacks by the Ku Klux Klan, terrorized African Americans who attempted to exercise their new rights. State governments found creative ways to circumvent the amendment's requirements, establishing segregation systems that would later be validated under the "separate but equal" doctrine.

The Supreme Court's early interpretations severely limited the amendment's scope. In the Slaughterhouse Cases of 1873, the Court effectively nullified the privileges or immunities clause by ruling that it protected only a narrow set of national citizenship rights. This decision prevented the clause from becoming the broad guarantee of civil rights that its framers had intended.

The Court's retreat from robust enforcement continued in United States v. Cruikshank (1876), which held that the Fourteenth Amendment did not empower Congress to punish private individuals who violated others' constitutional rights. This ruling severely hampered federal efforts to protect African Americans from organized violence and intimidation.

Perhaps most damaging was the Court's 1883 invalidation of the Civil Rights Act of 1875 in the Civil Rights Cases. The Court held that the Fourteenth Amendment only prohibited state discrimination, not private acts of racial exclusion. This decision gave constitutional blessing to the system of private segregation that would characterize American life for the next century.

These restrictive interpretations coincided with the broader collapse of Reconstruction. As federal troops withdrew from the South and northern public opinion tired of civil rights enforcement, states increasingly ignored the amendment's requirements. The rise of Jim Crow segregation demonstrated how the amendment's revolutionary potential had been temporarily defeated by a combination of judicial limitation, political exhaustion, and violent resistance.

Yet even in this period of retrenchment, the Fourteenth Amendment's fundamental principles remained embedded in constitutional law, waiting to be revived by future generations. African American activists and their allies continued to invoke its guarantees, laying the groundwork for the civil rights movement of the twentieth century.

The amendment's early years also saw its unexpected application to corporations, as the Supreme Court began interpreting the due process clause to protect business interests from state regulation. This development, while far from the amendment's original purpose, demonstrated its adaptability to changing circumstances and its potential to address various forms of state power.

The complex legacy of the Fourteenth Amendment's early period continues to influence constitutional law today. Its initial promise, subsequent limitation, and eventual revival provide crucial lessons about both the possibilities and challenges of using constitutional law to achieve social transformation. The amendment's early history reminds us that constitutional guarantees require sustained political will and vigilant enforcement to translate noble principles into lived reality.

Equal Protection: The Fourteenth Amendment's Evolution

The evolution of the Fourteenth Amendment's Equal Protection Clause represents one of the most dramatic transformations in American constitutional law, fundamentally reshaping the relationship between citizens and their government while establishing the legal foundation for civil rights advances that would unfold over more than a century.

The Supreme Court's early interpretations of equal protection proved devastatingly narrow. In Plessy v. Ferguson (1896), the Court upheld racial segregation under the infamous "separate but equal" doctrine, ruling that enforced separation of races did not violate equal protection as long as facilities were ostensibly equivalent. This ruling gave constitutional blessing to Jim Crow laws and established a framework of legalized discrimination that would persist until the mid-twentieth century.

Despite this severe setback, equal protection doctrine began showing signs of evolution even during the Plessy era. In Yick Wo v. Hopkins (1886), the Court struck down a San Francisco ordinance that was applied discriminatorily against Chinese laundry operators, establishing that facially neutral laws could violate equal protection if administered with discriminatory intent. This principle would later prove crucial in challenging various forms of racial discrimination.

The modern revolution in equal protection jurisprudence began with the Supreme Court's landmark decision in Brown v. Board of Education (1954). Chief Justice Earl Warren's unanimous opinion declared that separate educational facilities were inherently unequal, effectively overturning Plessy. The decision reflected both evolving social attitudes and new understanding of segregation's psychological impacts, demonstrated through social science research presented to the Court.

Brown's impact extended far beyond school desegregation, establishing a new framework for analyzing equal protection claims. The Court developed different levels of scrutiny for different types of discrimination. Classifications based on race or national origin became subject to "strict scrutiny," requiring government to show both a compelling interest and narrow tailoring of means to ends. Gender-based distinctions later received "intermediate scrutiny," while most other classifications faced only "rational basis" review.

The 1960s saw rapid expansion of equal protection principles. In Loving v. Virginia (1967), the Court struck down laws banning interracial marriage, recognizing that such restrictions violated both equal protection and fundamental rights. Cases like Baker v. Carr (1962) and Reynolds v. Sims (1964) extended equal protection to voting rights, establishing the principle of "one person, one vote" in legislative districting.

Gender equality emerged as a major focus of equal protection litigation in the 1970s. In Reed v. Reed (1971), the Court for the first time struck down a law discriminating based on sex, invalidating an Idaho statute preferring men over women as estate administrators. This opened the door to numerous challenges of gender-based classifications, led by advocates like Ruth Bader Ginsburg who strategically built precedents expanding women's legal equality.

The Court's approach to affirmative action highlighted both the evolution and complexity of equal protection doctrine. In Regents of the University of California v. Bakke (1978), the Court struck down rigid racial quotas while allowing consideration of race as one factor in admissions to promote diversity. Subsequent cases like Grutter v. Bollinger (2003) refined this framework, requiring periodic reassessment of the continuing need for race-conscious policies.

Equal protection analysis expanded beyond traditional categories to address new forms of discrimination. In Plyler v. Doe (1982), the Court protected undocumented children's right to public education. Romer v. Evans (1996) struck down a state constitutional amendment barring anti-discrimination protections for gay people, while United States v. Windsor (2013) and Obergefell v. Hodges (2015) extended equal protection principles to same-sex marriage.

The doctrine also evolved to address subtle forms of discrimination. Cases like Washington v. Davis (1976) established frameworks for analyzing policies that were neutral on their face but had discriminatory impacts, though the Court generally required proof of discriminatory intent rather than just disparate effects. This approach influenced everything from employment discrimination to environmental justice claims.

Modern equal protection jurisprudence continues grappling with complex questions of discrimination and remedy. Debates over affirmative action, voting rights, and LGBTQ+ equality demonstrate ongoing tension between formal equality and substantive fairness. Questions about algorithmic bias and artificial intelligence raise new challenges for identifying and addressing discrimination.

The clause's impact extends far beyond courtrooms, influencing legislation, administrative policy, and social attitudes. Equal protection principles shape everything from workplace regulations to school discipline policies. They provide both practical tools for challenging discrimination and moral authority for advancing equality.

This evolution reflects broader changes in American society's understanding of equality and discrimination. What began as a specific guarantee of racial equality has become a flexible tool for addressing various forms of arbitrary or unfair treatment by government. The clause's meaning continues to develop through interaction between courts, legislatures, and social movements.

The Equal Protection Clause's transformation demonstrates both the potential and limitations of constitutional provisions to drive social change. While court decisions alone cannot eliminate discrimination, they can provide crucial legal framework for broader movements toward equality. The clause's evolution from Plessy to Brown to Obergefell shows how constitutional meaning can grow to meet society's developing moral understanding.

Due Process Revolution: Fourteenth Amendment Transformed

The Due Process Revolution fundamentally transformed American constitutional law, extending federal protections to state actions and establishing new safeguards for individual rights. This dramatic expansion of the Fourteenth Amendment's Due Process Clause reshaped the relationship between citizens and government at all levels, creating the framework of civil liberties Americans enjoy today.

The revolution began with a seemingly technical legal distinction. The Bill of Rights originally restricted only federal power, leaving states free to regulate speech, religion, criminal procedure, and other fundamental rights as they saw fit. This limited scope stemmed from the Supreme Court's 1833 decision in Barron v. Baltimore, which explicitly held that the Bill of Rights did not apply to state governments.

The ratification of the Fourteenth Amendment in 1868 set the stage for change, though the transformation would take nearly a century to fully unfold. The amendment's Due Process Clause declared that no state shall "deprive any person of life, liberty, or property, without due process of law." These words echoed the Fifth Amendment's restriction on federal power, raising the question of whether they imposed similar substantive limits on state authority.

Early Supreme Court decisions took a narrow view, focusing primarily on procedural fairness rather than substantive rights. The Court's infamous 1873 Slaughterhouse Cases effectively gutted the amendment's Privileges or Immunities Clause, which many had viewed as the primary vehicle for applying federal rights protections to the states. This decision shifted focus to the Due Process Clause as the potential basis for expanding constitutional protections.

The concept of "substantive due process" emerged gradually through cases challenging state economic regulations. In Allgeyer v. Louisiana (1897), the Court recognized freedom of contract as a liberty protected by due process. This principle reached its apex in Lochner v. New York (1905), which struck down maximum working hours legislation as an unconstitutional interference with contractual freedom. While the Lochner era's protection of economic rights would eventually be repudiated, its recognition that due process protected substantive rights laid important groundwork.

The modern due process revolution began in earnest with Gitlow v. New York (1925), which suggested that First Amendment free speech protections might apply to states through the Fourteenth Amendment. This process of "selective incorporation" accelerated under the Warren Court, systematically applying most Bill of Rights protections to state governments. Cases like Mapp v. Ohio (1961) and Gideon v. Wainwright (1963) transformed criminal justice by requiring states to follow federal standards for search and seizure, right to counsel, and other procedural protections.

Beyond incorporating specific Bill of Rights provisions, the Due Process Clause became a source of independent rights protection. In Meyer v. Nebraska (1923) and Pierce v. Society of Sisters (1925), the Court recognized parents' fundamental right to direct their children's education. Skinner v. Oklahoma (1942) protected the right to procreate from forced sterilization laws. These decisions established that certain fundamental liberties received heightened constitutional protection from state interference.

The sexual privacy and reproductive rights cases marked another watershed. Griswold v. Connecticut (1965) struck down restrictions on contraception access, recognizing a constitutional right to privacy in intimate matters. This principle expanded dramatically in Roe v. Wade (1973), protecting abortion rights as an aspect of privacy and personal autonomy protected by due process. While controversial, these decisions established that due process liberty encompassed personal decisions about family, reproduction, and intimate relationships.

The doctrine continued evolving to address new rights claims. Moore v. City of East Cleveland (1977) protected extended family living arrangements from zoning restrictions. Cruzan v. Director, Missouri Department of Health (1990) recognized a right to refuse medical treatment. Lawrence v. Texas (2003) struck down sodomy laws, protecting sexual autonomy regardless of orientation. These cases demonstrated the clause's adaptability to changing social values and emerging liberty interests.

Procedural due process also underwent significant development. Cases like Goldberg v. Kelly (1970) established minimum procedures required before terminating government benefits. Matthews v. Eldridge (1976) created a flexible framework for determining what process was due in different contexts. These decisions recognized that new forms of government benefits and licenses had become vital to modern life, requiring appropriate procedural protections.

The due process revolution faced criticism from various quarters. Conservatives argued that courts were inventing rights without constitutional foundation. Originalists contended that incorporation distorted the amendment's original meaning. Others worried that expanding due process protections unduly restricted democratic decision making by state governments.

Yet the transformation proved remarkably durable. Even as the Court's composition changed, most due process protections remained intact. New rights continued receiving recognition, as in Obergefell v. Hodges (2015) protecting same sex marriage. The doctrine evolved to address modern challenges like digital privacy and genetic information.

The due process revolution's impact extended far beyond courtrooms. State governments reformed their procedures to meet constitutional requirements. Police departments changed arrest and interrogation practices. Schools modified disciplinary procedures.

Healthcare providers developed informed consent protocols. These practical changes demonstrated how constitutional doctrine could reshape everyday interactions between citizens and government.

Today's due process jurisprudence reflects both the revolution's achievements and continuing challenges. Questions persist about unenumerated rights, the proper balance between state and federal authority, and adaptation to technological change. Yet the core principle that states must respect fundamental rights and provide fair procedures has become deeply embedded in American law and society.

The due process revolution stands as one of the most significant transformations in American constitutional law, establishing protections that Americans now take for granted. Its evolution demonstrates how constitutional provisions can grow to meet society's developing understanding of liberty and justice, while providing practical tools for protecting individual rights against government overreach.

Voting Rights Begin: The Fifteenth Amendment Story

The ratification of the Fifteenth Amendment in 1870 marked a revolutionary moment in American democracy, extending voting rights to African American men and establishing for the first time that race could not be used to deny the right to vote. This milestone emerged from the tumultuous period of Reconstruction, when the nation grappled with redefining citizenship and equality in the aftermath of the Civil War.

The amendment's origins lay in the bitter political battles of Reconstruction. Despite the Fourteenth Amendment's broad guarantees of citizenship and equal protection, many states continued to deny African Americans the right to vote through various legal mechanisms. Republican leaders in Congress recognized that without voting rights, the promises of citizenship would remain hollow, and freed slaves would remain vulnerable to exploitation and discrimination.

The path to ratification proved contentious. Congressional debates revealed deep divisions not just between North and South, but among Republicans themselves. Some pushed for broader provisions addressing literacy tests and poll taxes, while others worried such measures would alienate moderate supporters. The final text represented a compromise, stating simply that voting rights could not be denied "on account of race, color, or previous condition of servitude."

Initial enforcement of the amendment showed promising results. Black voter registration and participation surged across the South. In states like South Carolina and Mississippi, African Americans were elected to local, state, and federal offices in unprecedented numbers.

This period of multiracial democracy, though brief, demonstrated the transformative potential of expanded suffrage.

However, the amendment's effectiveness soon faced severe challenges. As federal troops withdrew from the South and Reconstruction policies weakened, states began implementing various measures to circumvent the amendment's protections. Literacy tests, poll taxes, grandfather clauses, and complex registration requirements emerged as tools to disenfranchise African American voters while technically complying with the Fifteenth Amendment's literal text.

Violence and intimidation also played a crucial role in undermining the amendment's promise. The rise of the Ku Klux Klan and similar organizations created an atmosphere of terror that discouraged many African Americans from attempting to exercise their voting rights. Local law enforcement often turned a blind eye to such activities or actively participated in voter suppression.

The Supreme Court's narrow interpretation of the amendment further limited its impact. In United States v. Reese (1876), the Court struck down parts of the Enforcement Act of 1870, ruling that the Fifteenth Amendment only prohibited explicit racial discrimination in voting, not other measures that might disproportionately affect African Americans. This decision established a pattern of restrictive interpretation that would persist for decades.

The combination of legal obstacles, violence, and judicial restraint led to a dramatic decline in African American voting participation by the early 1900s. In many Southern states, registration rates fell to near zero. This disenfranchisement had profound consequences, enabling the establishment of Jim Crow segregation and ensuring that African Americans would have little voice in the political decisions affecting their lives.

Despite these setbacks, the Fifteenth Amendment remained a crucial constitutional foundation for later voting rights advances. Civil rights activists in the twentieth century repeatedly invoked its principles in challenging discriminatory voting practices. The amendment's clear prohibition of racial discrimination in voting provided legal and moral authority for the civil rights movement's voting rights campaigns.

The passage of the Voting Rights Act of 1965 finally gave the Fifteenth Amendment the enforcement mechanism it had long lacked. This landmark legislation prohibited discriminatory voting practices and established federal oversight of election procedures in states with histories of discrimination. The combination of constitutional principle and statutory enforcement led to dramatic increases in African American voter registration and participation.

Modern voting rights challenges continue to implicate the Fifteenth Amendment's protections. Debates over voter ID laws, polling place closures, and redistricting practices often raise questions about racial discrimination in voting. The Supreme Court's 2013 decision in Shelby County v. Holder, which struck down key provisions of the Voting Rights Act, sparked renewed controversy about the adequate protection of minority voting rights.

The amendment's legacy extends beyond race-based discrimination. Its establishment of federal power to protect voting rights helped pave the way for later expansions of suffrage through the Nineteenth, Twenty-fourth, and Twenty-sixth Amendments. It also established important principles about Congress's authority to enforce constitutional rights through appropriate legislation.

The Fifteenth Amendment's story illustrates both the possibilities and limitations of constitutional change. While its ratification represented a revolutionary expansion of democratic participation, its effectiveness ultimately depended on political will, enforcement mechanisms, and judicial interpretation. This complex history continues to inform contemporary debates about voting rights, racial equality, and the ongoing project of American democracy.

Today, as Americans continue to debate access to the ballot box, the Fifteenth Amendment's core principle that voting rights cannot be denied based on race remains vital. Its history reminds us that constitutional guarantees require vigilant protection and robust enforcement to fulfill their promise. The amendment stands as both a milestone in the expansion of American democracy and a reminder of the ongoing struggle to secure equal voting rights for all citizens.

Progressive Taxation: The Sixteenth Amendment Battle

The passage of the Sixteenth Amendment in 1913 fundamentally transformed the American tax system and the federal government's power to fund its operations. Before this watershed moment, the federal government relied primarily on tariffs and excise taxes for revenue, as the Supreme Court had previously ruled that a federal income tax violated the Constitution's requirement that direct taxes be apportioned among the states based on population.

The push for a federal income tax emerged from the Progressive Movement of the late nineteenth and early twentieth centuries. Progressives argued that the existing tax system placed an unfair burden on working Americans while allowing the wealthy to accumulate vast fortunes largely untaxed. The growing inequality of the Gilded Age, combined with the need for stable government revenue, created mounting pressure for tax reform.

The Supreme Court's 1895 decision in Pollock v. Farmers' Loan & Trust Company had struck down the Income Tax Act of 1894, ruling that taxes on income from property were direct taxes that had to be apportioned among the states. This decision effectively prevented any broad-based federal income tax, as apportionment would have made such a tax administratively impossible and politically unpalatable.

The campaign for a constitutional amendment gained momentum in the early 1900s, supported by both Progressive Republicans and Democrats. President William Howard Taft, though personally opposed to an income tax, recognized the growing popular demand and strategically supported the amendment to prevent more radical tax proposals. Corporate leaders, while generally opposing the amendment, found themselves unable to stem the tide of public opinion favoring tax reform.

Congressional debate over the amendment revealed deep philosophical divisions about the nature of taxation and federal power. Opponents warned that a federal income tax would give the government too much control over citizens' private affairs and could lead to excessive taxation. Supporters countered that the tax would create a fairer system and provide necessary revenue for an increasingly complex modern nation.

The final text of the amendment was remarkably simple: "The Congress shall have power to lay and collect taxes on incomes, from whatever source derived, without apportionment among the several States, and without regard to any census or enumeration." This straightforward language granted broad authority to Congress, avoiding specific limitations that might have restricted future tax policy.

State ratification proceeded relatively quickly, reflecting broad popular support for the measure. By 1913, the required three-fourths of states had ratified the amendment, marking a significant victory for Progressive reformers. Congress quickly passed implementing legislation, establishing the modern federal income tax system.

The immediate impact of the Sixteenth Amendment was modest by modern standards. The initial tax affected only about 1% of the population, with rates ranging from 1% to 7%. However, the amendment's importance grew dramatically during World War I, when the government used its new taxing power to fund the war effort. Tax rates increased significantly, and the number of Americans paying income tax expanded.

The amendment's long-term effects on American society and government have been profound. It enabled the creation of the modern administrative state by providing a reliable source of federal revenue. The income tax became the government's primary funding mechanism, supporting everything from national defense to social programs. The

Internal Revenue Service grew into a massive bureaucracy responsible for collecting and enforcing the increasingly complex tax code.

The progressive nature of the income tax system, with higher rates on higher incomes, became a key tool for addressing economic inequality. During the New Deal and World War II, top marginal tax rates reached as high as 94%, reflecting a dramatic shift in attitudes about taxation and wealth redistribution since the amendment's passage.

Supreme Court interpretations of the Sixteenth Amendment have generally upheld broad congressional power to tax income. The Court has defined "income" expansively and rejected various attempts to limit federal taxing authority. However, debates continue over what constitutes income and the extent of Congress's power to tax different types of economic activity.

The amendment has sparked ongoing political and economic debates. Conservatives have criticized the income tax as overly burdensome and called for simpler, flatter tax systems. Progressives have defended progressive taxation as necessary for social justice and government services. These debates reflect broader disagreements about the role of government and economic fairness.

The Sixteenth Amendment's legacy extends beyond taxation. It represents a crucial moment in the expansion of federal power and the government's role in economic management. The amendment enabled the creation of the modern welfare state and fundamentally altered the relationship between citizens and the federal government.

In recent decades, debates over tax reform have continued to reference the amendment's history and purpose. Proposals for alternative tax systems, from flat taxes to consumption taxes, must contend with both the constitutional framework established by the Sixteenth Amendment and the administrative infrastructure built upon it.

The story of the Sixteenth Amendment illustrates how constitutional change can reshape government power and social relations in fundamental ways. What began as a Progressive Era reform has become a cornerstone of modern American governance, enabling the federal government to fund an expansive range of activities and programs that would have been unimaginable to earlier generations.

People's Senate: Seventeenth Amendment Reform

The direct election of United States Senators stands as one of the most significant democratic reforms of the Progressive Era, fundamentally altering the relationship between citizens and their federal government. Before the Seventeenth Amendment's ratification in 1913, state legislatures elected senators, creating a system that reformers increasingly criticized as corrupt and unresponsive to popular will.

The original constitutional framework for selecting senators reflected the Founding Fathers' vision of the Senate as a deliberative body insulated from direct democratic pressures. State legislatures would choose senators, creating what James Madison described as a "necessary fence" against the passions of popular democracy. This indirect election system functioned relatively well in the early republic but began showing serious strains by the mid-nineteenth century.

As America industrialized and corporate power grew, the Senate selection process became increasingly tainted by corruption. Wealthy business interests found they could effectively buy Senate seats by influencing state legislators through bribes and political contributions. The infamous "millionaires' club" nickname for the Senate reflected public perception of the chamber as a bastion of privileged interests rather than popular representation.

Deadlocks in state legislatures presented another serious problem. Partisan divisions often prevented legislatures from agreeing on a senator, leaving states without full representation in Congress. Between 1891 and 1905, there were 45 such deadlocks in 20 different states. Delaware went without any Senate representation for four years due to legislative gridlock. These failures of the indirect election system fueled growing calls for reform.

The Progressive Movement seized upon direct election of senators as a key democratic reform. Progressive reformers argued that popular election would make senators more accountable to ordinary citizens and reduce corruption in the selection process. They connected senate reform to other democratic initiatives like primary elections, initiative and referendum, and women's suffrage.

Several states didn't wait for a constitutional amendment, developing various mechanisms to approximate direct election. Oregon pioneered the "Oregon System" in 1904, which allowed voters to indicate their senate preference in a non-binding primary. State legislators then faced intense pressure to follow the voters' choice. Other states adopted similar measures, creating a patchwork of selection methods that highlighted the need for uniform national reform.

The movement for direct election gained crucial momentum when muckraking journalists exposed sensational cases of senatorial corruption. David Graham Phillips' "Treason of the Senate" series in Cosmopolitan magazine revealed how corporate interests dominated senate selections, helping galvanize public support for reform. Progressive politicians like William Jennings Bryan and Robert La Follette became powerful advocates for the cause.

Opposition to the amendment came primarily from conservative senators and state political machines that benefited from the existing system. They argued that direct election would upset the federal balance and weaken states' rights. Southern opponents particularly feared that federal oversight of Senate elections might threaten white supremacy in their region.

After several failed attempts, Congress finally passed the amendment in 1912. The text was straightforward, providing for direct popular election of senators while maintaining each state's equal representation in the Senate. It also preserved the power of state governors to make temporary appointments to fill vacancies, though states could require special elections for such situations.

Ratification proceeded swiftly, reflecting broad public support for the reform. By April 1913, the necessary three-fourths of states had approved the amendment, marking a significant victory for Progressive democracy. The first direct Senate elections were held in 1914, beginning a new era in American political representation.

The immediate impact of the Seventeenth Amendment was significant. The social and economic composition of the Senate gradually shifted, with more middle-class professionals winning election. Corporate influence didn't disappear but had to operate more openly through campaign contributions and lobbying rather than direct manipulation of state legislators.

Over time, direct election transformed the nature of Senate campaigns and governance. Senators became more responsive to public opinion and more likely to champion popular causes. The need to appeal directly to voters led to more extensive campaigning and increased importance of media coverage and campaign funding. This created new challenges regarding money in politics but within a more democratic framework.

The amendment's effects rippled through the federal system. State legislatures lost their most important leverage over federal policy, accelerating the trend toward greater federal power. Some scholars argue this shift weakened federalism, while others contend it simply modernized the federal relationship for an interconnected industrial nation.

Modern critics of the Seventeenth Amendment, particularly among conservatives, argue that direct election has contributed to federal overreach and diminished states' rights. They contend that the original system of legislative selection better protected state interests and provided an important check on federal power. However, few seriously propose returning to indirect election.

The Seventeenth Amendment's legacy extends beyond its specific provisions for Senate selection. It represents a crucial victory for democratic reform and popular sovereignty, demonstrating how progressive movements can successfully change fundamental aspects of governmental structure. The amendment helped establish the principle that democratic legitimacy requires direct voter participation in selecting representatives at all levels.

Today, as debates continue about campaign finance reform, term limits, and the nature of representation, the Seventeenth Amendment stands as a reminder that even seemingly permanent features of American government can be changed through organized political action and constitutional amendment. Its history offers important lessons for contemporary reform movements seeking to make American democracy more responsive to popular will.

Noble Experiment: Eighteenth Amendment's Prohibition

The story of Prohibition stands as one of the most remarkable and ultimately unsuccessful experiments in American constitutional history. The Eighteenth Amendment, ratified in 1919, marked the first time the Constitution was used to restrict individual behavior rather than protect rights or modify governmental structure. This noble experiment, as Herbert Hoover later called it, represented the pinnacle of the temperance movement's influence and the beginning of its eventual downfall.

The roots of Prohibition stretch back to the early 19th century when religious reformers began linking alcohol consumption to social problems like poverty, domestic violence, and moral decay. The American Temperance Society, founded in 1826, grew rapidly, evolving from advocating moderation to demanding complete abstinence. By the 1850s, several states had experimented with prohibition laws, though most were eventually repealed or struck down by courts.

The Women's Christian Temperance Union, founded in 1874, transformed the movement by connecting alcohol prohibition to women's rights, child welfare, and social reform. Under the dynamic leadership of Frances Willard, the WCTU became the largest women's organization in American history, wielding significant political influence. The Anti-Saloon League, established in 1893, added sophisticated political organizing and single issue focus, making prohibition a decisive factor in local and state elections.

World War I provided the final push toward national prohibition. Anti German sentiment targeted breweries, many owned by German Americans. Wartime conservation measures restricted grain use for alcohol production. The movement successfully portrayed drinking as unpatriotic and saloons as centers of sedition. By 1917, the political momentum seemed unstoppable.

The amendment's text was deceptively simple. It prohibited the manufacture, sale, and transportation of intoxicating liquors while giving Congress and states concurrent power to enforce the ban. This straightforward language masked complex implementation challenges that would later prove insurmountable. Despite these potential difficulties, the amendment moved swiftly through Congress and state ratification, becoming law in just 13 months.

Prohibition's early days seemed promising to supporters. Alcohol consumption declined significantly, and some communities reported drops in crime and public drunkenness. Working class families reported having more money for necessities when wages weren't spent at saloons. Some former drinking establishments converted to soft drink parlors or other businesses.

However, problems quickly emerged. The Volstead Act, which provided enforcement mechanisms, proved controversial from the start. Its strict definition of intoxicating liquors and limited exceptions for medical and religious use created widespread resistance. Enforcement resources proved woefully inadequate for the massive task of policing the nation's drinking habits.

Underground drinking establishments, known as speakeasies, proliferated in cities across America. Bootlegging became a massive criminal enterprise, creating fortunes for organized crime figures like Al Capone. Corruption of law enforcement officials became endemic as bribes from bootleggers exceeded their modest salaries. Home brewing and bathtub gin production flourished, sometimes with deadly consequences from poorly made alcohol.

The amendment created unprecedented challenges to federal-state relations. While some states enthusiastically enforced prohibition, others effectively nullified it through non-enforcement. Federal agents often faced local hostility and non-cooperation. The strain on the judicial system became enormous as prohibition cases flooded the courts.

Cultural resistance to prohibition grew steadily through the 1920s. Urban sophisticates made drinking fashionable, while working class Americans resented the law's intrusion into personal liberty. Women, who had been crucial to prohibition's passage, increasingly saw the law as creating more problems than it solved. The emergence of the flapper culture directly challenged temperance movement values.

Economic arguments against prohibition gained force during the Great Depression. Potential tax revenue from legal alcohol sales appealed to cash-strapped governments. Job creation from a revived brewing and distilling industry attracted union support. Business leaders who had once backed prohibition now saw it as an impediment to economic recovery.

The amendment's failure ultimately stemmed from its attempt to legislate personal morality on a national scale. It represented an overreach of progressive reform impulses, trying to solve complex social problems through simple prohibition. The law proved unenforceable without widespread public support and created more problems than it solved.

Prohibition's legacy extends beyond its eventual repeal. It demonstrated the limitations of using constitutional amendments for social reform and the dangers of criminalizing widely desired goods. The growth of organized crime during this period continued to influence American society long after repeal. The period also transformed American drinking patterns, establishing cocktail culture and changing the role of drinking establishments in community life.

The Eighteenth Amendment stands as a cautionary tale about the limits of constitutional reform and the importance of building genuine social consensus rather than merely achieving political victory. Its failure highlighted the need to address social problems through more nuanced approaches than outright prohibition. Yet it also demonstrated the powerful capacity of American society to recognize and correct constitutional mistakes through the amendment process itself.

Modern debates over drug policy and other moral issues often reference the prohibition experience. The amendment's history offers important lessons about the challenges of legislating morality and the unintended consequences of criminalizing popular behaviors. It remains a fascinating chapter in the ongoing story of how Americans use and sometimes misuse their power to amend the Constitution.

Women's Suffrage: The Nineteenth Amendment Victory

The fight for women's suffrage represents one of the longest and most significant battles in American constitutional history, culminating in the ratification of the Nineteenth Amendment in 1920. This transformative addition to the Constitution marked the single largest expansion of voting rights in American history, enfranchising approximately half the nation's adult population with the simple declaration that voting rights could not be denied on account of sex.

The roots of the women's suffrage movement stretch back to the earliest days of the Republic. Abigail Adams famously urged her husband John to "remember the ladies" during the Constitutional Convention, though her plea went unheeded. The 1848 Seneca Falls Convention, organized by Elizabeth Cady Stanton and Lucretia Mott, marked the formal beginning of the organized suffrage movement. Their Declaration of Sentiments, modeled on the Declaration of Independence, boldly asserted women's equality and right to the vote.

The Civil War temporarily suspended suffrage activism as many women focused on supporting the Union cause and abolition. The post war period brought bitter disappointment when the Fourteenth and Fifteenth Amendments explicitly introduced the word "male" into the Constitution and extended voting rights to African American men while excluding women of all races. This setback created a rift in the suffrage movement, with some activists like Susan B. Anthony and Elizabeth Cady Stanton opposing the Fifteenth Amendment's ratification unless it included women.

The movement adopted multiple strategies in the following decades. Some suffragists pursued a state by state approach, achieving notable successes particularly in western states. Wyoming granted women full voting rights in 1869 while still a territory, maintaining them when achieving statehood in 1890. Colorado, Utah, and Idaho followed by 1896. Other activists focused on challenging male only voting restrictions in court, though the Supreme Court consistently ruled against them, most notably in Minor v. Happersett in 1875.

The emergence of a new generation of suffrage leaders in the early 20th century brought fresh energy and tactics to the movement. Carrie Chapman Catt reorganized the National American Woman Suffrage Association into an efficient political machine, while Alice Paul's more militant National Woman's Party adopted aggressive protest strategies learned from British suffragettes. Paul organized the first pickets of the White House, leading to arrests and hunger strikes that drew national attention to the cause.

World War I proved crucial to the suffrage campaign's final success. Women's contributions to the war effort undermined arguments about their inability to participate in civic life. President Woodrow Wilson, initially opposed to federal action on suffrage, gradually shifted his position, eventually supporting the amendment as a war measure essential to making the world "safe for democracy." Suffragists effectively argued that denying women the vote while fighting for democracy abroad represented dangerous hypocrisy.

The amendment's path through Congress proved challenging despite growing support. The House of Representatives passed it in 1918, but the Senate initially rejected it by two votes. A second attempt in 1919 finally succeeded, sending the amendment to the states for ratification. The ensuing campaign demonstrated the movement's sophisticated political organization, as suffrage supporters pressured state legislators across the country.

Tennessee became the decisive thirty sixth state to ratify in August 1920, following a dramatic vote that hinged on twenty four year old Harry Burn. The young legislator had planned to vote against ratification until receiving a letter from his mother urging him to support women's suffrage. His last minute switch in favor of the amendment provided the final vote needed for ratification.

The amendment's impact transformed American politics far beyond simply allowing women to vote. Political parties had to adapt their campaigns and platforms to appeal to female voters. Women began running for and winning public office in unprecedented numbers. Issues like child labor, public health, and education gained greater prominence on political agendas as women exercised their new political power.

The victory, however, remained incomplete for many women of color who faced continued disenfranchisement through state voting restrictions targeting racial minorities. Poll taxes, literacy tests, and other discriminatory measures effectively denied many African American, Hispanic, and Native American women their constitutional right to vote for decades after the Nineteenth Amendment's ratification.

The suffrage movement's success provided a model for future civil rights campaigns, demonstrating how persistent organizing, multiple tactical approaches, and building broad coalitions could achieve constitutional change. The movement developed sophisticated political strategies, mastered public relations, and effectively leveraged changing social conditions to achieve its goals.

The amendment's ratification represented not just a victory for women's rights but a fundamental shift in American democracy. It completed the transformation of voting from a privilege limited to property owning white men to a universal right of citizenship. This expansion of democracy strengthened American institutions by making them more representative and legitimate.

Today, the Nineteenth Amendment stands as a testament to the power of organized civic action to achieve constitutional change. Its history reminds us that fundamental rights often must be fought for over generations, requiring both persistent dedication and tactical flexibility. The women's suffrage movement demonstrated that determined citizens can overcome even deeply entrenched opposition to expand American democracy.

The amendment's legacy continues to influence contemporary debates about voting rights and democratic participation. It serves as both an inspiration for those seeking to expand political rights and a reminder that constitutional victories must be vigilantly protected to ensure their promises are fully realized for all Americans.

Lame Duck Reform: Twentieth Amendment Changes

The Twentieth Amendment, ratified in 1933, addressed a peculiar quirk in American governance that had persisted since the nation's founding: the "lame duck" period. This extended transition between election and inauguration had created numerous problems throughout American history, leading to what became known as the Lame Duck Amendment.

In the nation's early years, the lengthy transition period made practical sense. Travel was slow, and officials needed time to arrange their affairs and make the journey to Washington. The original Constitution set March 4 as the date for presidential inaugurations and the beginning of new congressional terms, creating a four month gap after November elections during which defeated officials remained in office.

By the twentieth century, this arrangement had become not just unnecessary but potentially dangerous. Advances in transportation and communication had eliminated the practical need for such a long transition, while the complexities of modern governance made the extended lame duck period increasingly problematic. Defeated officials, no longer accountable to voters, could make significant decisions affecting their successors.

The dangers of this system became particularly apparent during the economic crisis of 1932-33. Herbert Hoover, defeated in the November 1932 election, remained president during crucial months of the Great Depression. Franklin D. Roosevelt, though already elected, had no official power to address the banking crisis and economic collapse. The nation essentially remained in limbo while an outgoing administration, rejected by voters, retained full authority during a critical period.

Senator George Norris of Nebraska emerged as the amendment's primary champion. A progressive Republican, Norris had witnessed numerous instances of lame duck congressional sessions making controversial decisions without accountability. He first introduced a resolution to change the transition timeline in 1923, beginning a nearly decade long effort to reform the system.

The amendment's path through Congress reflected broad bipartisan recognition of the problem, though debate continued over specific details. Some worried that shortening the transition period too much might complicate the electoral college process or create problems in close elections requiring recounts. Others argued for an even shorter transition period, pointing to parliamentary systems where power transfers occurred almost immediately after elections.

The final version of the amendment moved presidential inaugurations to January 20 and the beginning of congressional terms to January 3. This compromise provided enough time for election certification and transition planning while significantly reducing the lame duck period. The amendment also clarified presidential succession rules in case of death during the transition period, addressing concerns that had existed since the founding.

State ratification proceeded relatively quickly, reflecting widespread agreement about the need for reform. Unlike more controversial amendments, the Twentieth faced little organized opposition. Most debates focused on technical details rather than the fundamental goal of reducing the lame duck period. The amendment achieved ratification in just 11 months, becoming part of the Constitution on January 23, 1933.

The amendment's impact extended beyond simply changing dates. It fundamentally altered the dynamics of political transitions in American government. The shortened period created greater pressure for efficient transfers of power but also reduced opportunities for mischief by defeated officials. Modern presidential transitions began preparing months before elections, developing detailed plans for either outcome.

The reform also affected congressional dynamics. The amendment eliminated the traditional "short session" of Congress that had occurred between December and March in election years. These sessions had often been dominated by defeated members with little accountability to voters, sometimes passing controversial legislation or making appointments that their successors opposed.

The Twentieth Amendment demonstrated how constitutional change could address practical problems in governmental operations. Unlike amendments focused on individual rights or major social changes, it represented a technical reform aimed at improving governmental efficiency and accountability. Its success showed how the Constitution could be updated to reflect changing technological and social conditions.

Modern scholars have noted that while the amendment significantly improved the transition process, some lame duck issues persist. The period between election and inauguration, though shorter, still allows defeated officials to make important decisions. Some have advocated for further reforms, though most agree the current system represents a reasonable balance between practical needs and democratic accountability.

The amendment's history also illustrates how constitutional change often responds to specific historical circumstances. The Great Depression crisis highlighted the problems with extended transitions, creating momentum for reform that might otherwise have taken longer to achieve. This pattern of crisis driving constitutional change would repeat throughout American history.

Today, the Twentieth Amendment's provisions are largely taken for granted, its changes having become standard features of American political transitions. Yet its passage marked an important step in modernizing American governance, adapting constitutional structures to twentieth century realities. The amendment stands as an example of how the Constitution can be reformed to address practical problems while maintaining fundamental democratic principles.

The reform's success in smoothing governmental transitions has influenced modern practices far beyond its specific provisions. Presidential transition teams now begin work months before elections, and modern communications allow for virtually instantaneous transfer of information between outgoing and incoming administrations. While these practices aren't mandated by the amendment, they reflect its spirit of ensuring efficient and democratic transfers of power.

End of Prohibition: Twenty-First Amendment Repeal

The repeal of Prohibition stands as one of the most dramatic reversals in American constitutional history. The Twenty First Amendment, ratified in 1933, marked the first and only time an entire constitutional amendment was repealed, ending America's grand experiment with nationwide alcohol prohibition.

The path to repeal began almost as soon as Prohibition took effect. While the Eighteenth Amendment's supporters had promised a new era of moral and social improvement, the reality proved far different. Instead of eliminating alcohol consumption, Prohibition drove it underground, creating a vast network of speakeasies, bootleggers, and organized crime. Cities saw a surge in violence as criminal organizations fought to control the lucrative illegal liquor trade.

Enforcement proved nearly impossible. The federal government lacked sufficient resources to police the entire nation's drinking habits, while many state and local authorities showed little enthusiasm for the task. Corrupt officials often protected illegal operations in exchange for bribes. Meanwhile, ordinary citizens regularly flouted the law, viewing alcohol prohibition as an unreasonable infringement on personal liberty.

The Great Depression dealt the final blow to Prohibition's remaining support. As unemployment soared and tax revenues plunged, many began to see legalized alcohol as both an economic opportunity and a potential source of government revenue. The argument that the nation could no longer afford to suppress a potential source of jobs and tax dollars proved particularly persuasive.

Pauline Sabin emerged as a surprising but effective leader of the repeal movement. A Republican socialite who had initially supported Prohibition, Sabin became convinced that the law had created more problems than it solved. She founded the Women's Organization for National Prohibition Reform, which grew to over 1.5 million members. Her involvement helped counter the traditional image of Prohibition as a women's issue, as many women's groups had been among the original supporters of the Eighteenth Amendment.

The repeal movement faced significant challenges. The powerful Anti Saloon League, which had spearheaded the drive for Prohibition, remained committed to defending it. Many rural and southern states strongly supported continuing Prohibition, viewing repeal as a threat to traditional values. Constitutional amendments require broad national consensus, and early repeal efforts struggled to build sufficient support.

The 1932 election proved decisive. Franklin D. Roosevelt campaigned on a platform supporting repeal, while the Democratic Party made it a major campaign issue. Their landslide victory demonstrated shifting public opinion and provided crucial political momentum for the repeal effort.

The Twenty First Amendment's structure reflected lessons learned from the Prohibition experience. Its first section simply repealed the Eighteenth Amendment. The second section, however, gave states broad authority to regulate alcohol within their borders. This compromise helped secure support from states that wished to remain dry, as they could maintain prohibition at the state level.

The amendment's ratification process broke new ground. Instead of following the traditional route of ratification by state legislatures, Congress chose to require state conventions. This approach, used for the first and only time in constitutional history, was designed to better reflect popular opinion and bypass state legislatures still influenced by rural prohibitionist sentiment.

The ratification conventions moved with unprecedented speed. Despite the complex process of selecting delegates and organizing conventions, the entire amendment was ratified in less than a year. Utah became the 36th state to ratify on December 5, 1933, marking the official end of national Prohibition.

The amendment's aftermath reshaped American alcohol regulation. Most states established comprehensive systems for controlling alcohol sales and distribution. The three tier system separating producers, distributors, and retailers became standard, designed to prevent the vertical integration that had characterized the pre Prohibition era. States adopted varying approaches, from near total control through state stores to relatively liberal licensing systems.

The Twenty First Amendment's second section has generated ongoing legal controversy. Courts have struggled to balance state authority over alcohol with other constitutional principles, particularly the Commerce Clause. Questions about direct wine shipments, interstate alcohol sales, and state regulatory powers continue to generate litigation and debate.

The repeal of Prohibition offers important lessons about constitutional change. It demonstrates how amendments can have unintended consequences and how public opinion can shift dramatically over time. The experience made future reformers more cautious about using constitutional amendments to address social issues, suggesting that such changes might better be handled through regular legislation.

The amendment also illustrated the Constitution's capacity for self correction. When an experiment in social reform proved unsuccessful, the democratic process provided a mechanism for reversal. This flexibility helped maintain the Constitution's legitimacy even as it acknowledged a significant policy failure.

Modern America still grapples with the amendment's legacy. States continue to maintain varying degrees of alcohol regulation, creating a complex patchwork of laws. The tension between state and federal authority over alcohol regulation remains a source of legal uncertainty. Meanwhile, debates over the regulation of other substances often reference the Prohibition experience, either as a cautionary tale or a source of lessons for current policy.

The Twenty First Amendment stands as a reminder that constitutional change can move in multiple directions. While most amendments expand federal power or individual rights, this one restored authority to states and ended a failed national policy. Its unique status as the only repealing amendment makes it a fascinating case study in how the Constitution adapts to changing social and political circumstances.

Term Limits: Twenty-Second Amendment Politics

The Twenty Second Amendment, ratified in 1951, marked a significant shift in American presidential power by formally limiting presidents to two terms in office. While this restriction had been an unwritten rule for most of American history, following George Washington's example, Franklin D. Roosevelt's unprecedented four terms prompted a movement to codify presidential term limits in the Constitution.

The push for a presidential term limit amendment gained momentum in the aftermath of World War II. Republicans, who had opposed Roosevelt's long tenure, led the charge, arguing that extended presidential service threatened democratic principles and risked establishing quasi-monarchical power in the executive branch. The amendment's supporters frequently invoked Washington's voluntary two-term limit as evidence that the founders had never intended presidents to serve indefinitely.

The political context of the amendment's passage reflected the complex dynamics of post-war America. While Roosevelt had died in 1945, concern about another president potentially matching his tenure remained strong among conservatives. The Republican-controlled 80th Congress made the amendment a priority, viewing it as a way to prevent future Democratic presidents from building the kind of long-term coalition that Roosevelt had maintained through the New Deal and war years.

The amendment's drafting process revealed competing visions of presidential power. Some advocates pushed for a single six-year term, arguing this would free presidents from reelection pressures. Others proposed allowing two four-year terms but spacing them apart to prevent consecutive service. The final version settled on a maximum of two terms, whether consecutive or not, plus a maximum of two years of a previous president's term if succession occurred.

Opposition to the amendment came primarily from Democrats, who viewed it as a partisan attack on Roosevelt's legacy. They argued that voters should retain the right to keep effective presidents in office, particularly during times of crisis. Some critics pointed out that the amendment might weaken presidents serving their second term, as they would become "lame ducks" immediately after reelection.

The ratification process moved relatively quickly by constitutional standards, taking less than four years. State legislatures generally split along party lines, with Republican-controlled states moving swiftly to approve the amendment while Democratic-controlled states often opposed it. Minnesota became the 36th state to ratify on February 27, 1951, marking the amendment's formal adoption.

The amendment's specific provisions created some interesting constitutional questions. It clarified that no person could be elected president more than twice, and no one who had served more than two years of another president's term could be elected more than once. This careful wording addressed various succession scenarios while maintaining the basic two-term principle.

Implementation of the amendment raised several technical issues. Questions arose about whether it applied to Harry Truman, who was president when it was ratified. The amendment specifically exempted the sitting president, allowing Truman to run again if he chose, though he ultimately decided not to seek another term in 1952.

The Twenty Second Amendment has significantly influenced presidential politics in the decades since its ratification. Second-term presidents, knowing they cannot seek reelection, often focus on foreign policy and their historical legacy rather than domestic political battles. This pattern has led to discussions about whether the amendment effectively weakens the presidency during second terms.

The amendment has also affected presidential succession planning. Vice presidents who assume the presidency must carefully calculate how much of their predecessor's term they can serve while maintaining eligibility for two full terms of their own. This mathematical consideration has influenced decisions about when and whether to seek the presidency after succession.

Critics of the amendment have periodically called for its repeal, arguing that it unnecessarily restricts voter choice and reduces presidential accountability in second terms. Some point to parliamentary democracies where leaders can serve as long as they maintain popular support. However, serious efforts to repeal the amendment have never gained significant traction.

The amendment's impact extends beyond its direct effects on presidential terms. It has influenced how presidents approach their time in office, often creating a race to accomplish major initiatives before becoming a lame duck. Second-term presidents frequently face diminished influence with Congress, as legislators look ahead to the next administration.

Modern discussions of the Twenty Second Amendment often focus on its relationship to democratic principles. Supporters argue it prevents the accumulation of excessive executive power and ensures regular political turnover. Critics contend it artificially limits democratic choice and creates unnecessary inefficiencies in government operations.

The amendment has also shaped presidential legacy building. Modern presidents, knowing they face a maximum of eight years in office, often begin planning their post-presidential careers and legacy projects early in their second terms. This has led to the development of elaborate presidential library systems and post-presidential foundations.

The Twenty Second Amendment stands as a testament to how specific historical circumstances can prompt constitutional change.

Roosevelt's unprecedented four terms created concerns about executive power that permanently altered the American presidency. While the amendment's immediate political context reflected post-war partisan dynamics, its effects have become a fundamental feature of American democracy, shaping how presidents govern and how the nation thinks about executive power.

DC Rights: Twenty-Third Amendment's Capital Story

The Twenty Third Amendment, ratified in 1961, marked a significant milestone in American democracy by finally granting presidential electors to the District of Columbia. Before this amendment, residents of the nation's capital existed in a peculiar state of democratic limbo, unable to participate in presidential elections despite living at the very seat of federal power.

The story of DC voting rights begins with the creation of the federal district itself. The Constitution's framers established a federal district under Congress's exclusive control, but they failed to address the political rights of its residents. This oversight became increasingly problematic as the District's population grew. By the mid-20th century, Washington DC had more residents than several states, yet its citizens could not vote for president or vice president.

The push for the Twenty Third Amendment gained momentum during the civil rights era of the 1950s. Advocates highlighted the irony of American democracy denying voting rights to citizens living in the shadow of the Capitol dome. The district's large African American population made the voting rights issue particularly poignant, as it intersected with broader civil rights struggles of the era. Critics of DC disenfranchisement often pointed out that American soldiers from the District could die fighting for democracy abroad while lacking basic democratic rights at home.

Congress began serious consideration of the amendment in 1960, with broad bipartisan support emerging for the measure. The proposal carefully balanced competing interests by granting the District electoral votes while limiting its influence. Under the amendment, DC would receive the number of electors it would be entitled to if it were a state, but no more than the least populous state. This effectively meant three electoral votes, corresponding to two senators and one representative.

The ratification process moved relatively quickly, reflecting the amendment's broad acceptance as a matter of basic fairness. State legislatures across the country recognized the fundamental injustice of denying presidential voting rights to American citizens solely because they lived in the federal district. The amendment was ratified on March 29, 1961, allowing District residents to participate in their first presidential election in 1964.

Implementation of the amendment required Congress to pass enabling legislation, which it did through the District of Columbia Election Act. This law established procedures for presidential elections in DC, including voter registration requirements and the method of choosing electors. The district's first presidential electors cast their votes for Lyndon Johnson in 1964, marking a historic moment in the expansion of American democracy.

The Twenty Third Amendment's impact extended beyond simply allowing DC residents to vote for president. It represented a significant symbolic victory in the ongoing struggle for full citizenship rights for District residents. The amendment's passage encouraged advocates to push for additional political rights, including congressional representation and local self-government. These efforts led to the passage of the Home Rule Act in 1973, granting DC limited local autonomy.

However, the amendment also highlighted the continuing limitations on District democracy. While it provided for presidential electors, it did not grant DC voting representation in Congress or full state status. This partial solution to DC's democratic deficit has fueled ongoing debates about the district's political status, including proposals for statehood or retrocession to Maryland.

The amendment's implementation revealed some unique aspects of DC's political character. The District has voted overwhelmingly

Democratic in every presidential election since gaining electoral votes, reflecting its urban, predominantly liberal population. This consistent voting pattern has influenced discussions about potential changes to DC's status, with partisan considerations often shaping debates about further expansions of District voting rights.

The Twenty Third Amendment also raised interesting questions about the nature of representation in American democracy. Unlike states, whose electoral votes reflect their congressional delegation, DC's electoral votes exist solely by constitutional grant. This unusual arrangement has prompted discussions about whether the amendment's approach might serve as a model for addressing other representation challenges in American democracy.

The amendment's legacy continues to evolve as debates about DC voting rights persist. While it represented a significant step forward, many argue it did not go far enough in addressing the fundamental democratic rights of District residents. The continuing lack of congressional voting representation has led to various protest movements, including DC's adoption of the slogan "Taxation Without Representation" on its license plates.

Modern interpretations of the Twenty Third Amendment often focus on its relationship to broader questions of democratic participation and representation. Scholars and activists frequently cite it as both a success story in expanding voting rights and a reminder of unfinished business in American democracy. The amendment's history offers insights into how constitutional change can address democratic deficits while also highlighting the challenges of achieving full political equality.

The experience of implementing the Twenty Third Amendment has influenced contemporary discussions about potential changes to DC's status. Statehood advocates often point to the smooth integration of DC into presidential elections as evidence that further expansions of District political rights would strengthen American democracy.

Opponents argue that the amendment struck the right balance, providing presidential voting rights while maintaining the district's unique constitutional status.

The Twenty Third Amendment stands as a testament to America's capacity to recognize and correct democratic deficiencies, even if incompletely. It represents both the promise and limitations of constitutional change in addressing fundamental questions of citizenship and representation. As debates about DC's political status continue, the amendment remains a crucial milestone in the ongoing evolution of American democracy.

Poll Tax Battle: Twenty-Fourth Amendment Victory

The fight against poll taxes in American elections represents one of the most direct confrontations with systemic voter suppression in the nation's history. The Twenty Fourth Amendment, ratified in 1964, finally abolished this insidious barrier to voting in federal elections, marking a crucial victory in the larger civil rights struggle of the 1960s.

Poll taxes emerged in the late 19th century as part of a broader strategy to disenfranchise African American voters and poor whites in the South. These taxes required citizens to pay a fee before they could cast their ballot, typically ranging from one to two dollars annually. While this might seem a modest sum today, it represented a significant burden for many poor Americans, especially when states required citizens to pay accumulated back taxes before voting.

The practice became particularly widespread after the adoption of new state constitutions throughout the South between 1890 and 1908. These constitutions implemented poll taxes alongside other voting restrictions like literacy tests and grandfather clauses. The taxes proved remarkably effective at suppressing voter participation. In Mississippi, for example, voter turnout dropped from 130,000 in 1876 to just 60,000 in 1892 after the implementation of poll taxes.

Early challenges to poll taxes faced significant obstacles. The Supreme Court initially upheld their constitutionality in Breedlove v. Suttles (1937), ruling that poll taxes did not violate the Fourteenth or Nineteenth Amendments. The Court's decision reflected the prevailing view that voting qualifications remained primarily under state control, despite federal constitutional protections.

The movement to abolish poll taxes gained momentum during World War II, as the contradiction between fighting fascism abroad while maintaining discriminatory voting practices at home became increasingly apparent. President Franklin D. Roosevelt spoke out against poll taxes, arguing they were incompatible with democratic principles. Civil rights organizations like the NAACP made abolishing poll taxes a key priority, viewing them as part of the broader struggle against Jim Crow laws.

Congressional efforts to eliminate poll taxes through legislation repeatedly failed during the 1940s and 1950s, largely due to Southern opposition. Bills passed the House of Representatives on five separate occasions but died in the Senate, where Southern senators used the filibuster to block action. This legislative deadlock eventually convinced advocates that a constitutional amendment would be necessary.

President John F. Kennedy endorsed the anti-poll tax amendment as part of his civil rights agenda. The proposal moved through Congress in 1962, with supporters arguing that poll taxes violated fundamental democratic principles and disproportionately affected minority voters. Southern opponents claimed the amendment infringed on states' rights and exceeded federal authority over election procedures.

The ratification process reflected changing national attitudes toward voting rights. Northern and Western states quickly approved the amendment, while Southern states largely opposed it. Virginia, which had vigorously defended its poll tax, became a focal point of the debate. The state's resistance highlighted the continuing struggle between federal civil rights initiatives and state-level opposition to racial equality.

When ratified in 1964, the Twenty Fourth Amendment prohibited poll taxes in federal elections. The amendment's specific focus on federal elections reflected a political compromise, leaving states free to maintain poll taxes in state elections. However, this limitation proved temporary, as the Supreme Court later ruled in

Harper v. Virginia Board of Elections (1966) that state poll taxes violated the Equal Protection Clause of the Fourteenth Amendment.

The amendment's impact extended beyond its immediate effect on voting practices. It represented a significant federal intervention in election procedures traditionally controlled by states, setting important precedents for later voting rights legislation. The success of the anti-poll tax movement also encouraged civil rights activists pushing for broader reforms, contributing to the momentum that led to the Voting Rights Act of 1965.

Implementation of the Twenty Fourth Amendment revealed the persistent nature of voting barriers. Some states attempted to replace poll taxes with other requirements designed to limit minority voting. These efforts prompted ongoing legal battles and highlighted the need for comprehensive federal voting rights protection.

The amendment's legacy continues to influence contemporary debates about voting rights and access to the ballot. Modern controversies over voter ID laws, registration requirements, and polling place accessibility often echo earlier debates about poll taxes. Advocates frequently cite the Twenty Fourth Amendment when challenging practices they view as creating financial barriers to voting.

The poll tax amendment also demonstrates the incremental nature of constitutional change. While it addressed one specific barrier to voting, it formed part of a larger process of expanding and protecting voting rights that continues today. Its passage reflected growing national recognition that economic status should not determine political participation.

Today, the Twenty Fourth Amendment stands as a reminder of both the progress made in securing voting rights and the continuing challenges in ensuring equal access to the ballot. Its history offers important lessons about the role of constitutional amendments in advancing civil rights and the persistent nature of efforts to restrict voting access through economic means.

The amendment's focus on removing financial barriers to voting remains relevant as debates continue about various election-related costs, from voter ID requirements to the accessibility of polling places. Its principles inform ongoing discussions about how to ensure that economic status does not determine political participation in American democracy.

Presidential Succession Crisis: Twenty-Fifth Amendment

The Twenty Fifth Amendment, ratified in 1967, emerged from one of the most traumatic events in American history: the assassination of President John F. Kennedy. While the nation had previously experienced presidential deaths in office, Kennedy's sudden loss exposed dangerous gaps in the constitutional provisions for presidential succession and incapacity that demanded immediate attention.

Before the Twenty Fifth Amendment, the Constitution's only guidance on presidential succession came from Article II, Section 1, Clause 6, which was remarkably vague about several crucial scenarios. While it established that the Vice President would take over in case of the President's death, removal, or resignation, it failed to address temporary presidential disability or specify whether the Vice President became President or merely acted as President. The text was also silent on how to fill a vice presidential vacancy, which had occurred sixteen times before 1967.

The assassination of President Kennedy brought these constitutional ambiguities into sharp focus. When Kennedy died, Vice President Lyndon Johnson assumed the presidency, leaving the vice presidency vacant for fourteen months until the next election. This dangerous gap in leadership during the height of the Cold War concerned many lawmakers and constitutional scholars. Moreover, if Johnson had become incapacitated during this period, the presidential succession would have fallen to the Speaker of the House, raising questions about partisan changes in executive leadership.

The historical record contained troubling precedents of presidential incapacity being handled inconsistently. When President James Garfield was shot in 1881, he lingered for eighty days, unable to perform his duties, yet no formal transfer of power occurred. Similarly, after President Woodrow Wilson suffered a severe stroke in 1919, his wife and closest advisers essentially ran the executive branch in secret for months, with no constitutional mechanism to transfer power temporarily to Vice President Thomas Marshall.

The push for what would become the Twenty Fifth Amendment began almost immediately after Kennedy's assassination. Senator Birch Bayh of Indiana, then chairman of the Senate Subcommittee on Constitutional Amendments, took the lead in drafting the amendment. Bayh worked closely with the American Bar Association and received input from former Presidents Eisenhower and Truman, as well as then-President Johnson.

The amendment addressed four specific scenarios. Section 1 codified the traditional practice that the Vice President becomes President upon the death, resignation, or removal of the President. Section 2 created a mechanism for filling vice presidential vacancies through presidential nomination and congressional confirmation. Section 3 allowed for voluntary transfer of presidential power to the Vice President during temporary disabilities. Most controversially, Section 4 established procedures for involuntary removal of presidential powers when the President is unable or unwilling to recognize their own incapacity.

The debate over the amendment revealed deep concerns about maintaining democratic legitimacy while ensuring governmental stability. Some lawmakers worried about potential abuse of the incapacity provisions, while others argued for even stronger measures. The final text represented a careful balance between competing interests, requiring broad consensus for involuntary removal of presidential powers while ensuring clear procedures for necessary transitions.

Ratification proceeded relatively quickly, reflecting broad bipartisan agreement on the amendment's necessity. State legislatures recognized the importance of closing these constitutional gaps, particularly given Cold War tensions and the nuclear age's demands for clear command authority. The amendment became part of the Constitution on February 10, 1967.

The Twenty Fifth Amendment's provisions have been invoked several times since ratification. Section 2 was used twice in the 1970s, first when Gerald Ford replaced Spiro Agnew as Vice President, and then when Nelson Rockefeller replaced Ford after he succeeded to the presidency following Richard Nixon's resignation. Section 3 has been used for brief periods during presidential medical procedures, including when Ronald Reagan underwent cancer surgery in 1985 and when George W. Bush had colonoscopies in 2002 and 2007.

Section 4, the amendment's most dramatic provision, has never been formally invoked, though its potential use was discussed during the Reagan administration after the assassination attempt in 1981 and during the final days of the Trump administration following the January 6, 2021 Capitol riot. These discussions highlight the amendment's continuing relevance while also demonstrating the high threshold required for its most serious provisions.

The amendment's impact extends beyond its specific applications. It has helped stabilize American democracy by providing clear procedures for presidential succession and disability, reducing uncertainty during potential leadership crises. Its provisions have become part of continuity of government planning and influence how the executive branch prepares for various contingencies.

Modern discussions of the Twenty Fifth Amendment often focus on its potential application to scenarios its drafters might not have anticipated, such as presidential mental health issues or gradual cognitive decline. These debates reflect the challenge of applying constitutional provisions to evolving circumstances while maintaining their fundamental principles.

The amendment also raises broader questions about democratic governance and executive power. Its procedures for determining presidential inability require delicate balancing between medical expertise, political judgment, and democratic legitimacy. The involvement of both executive branch officials and Congress in these decisions reflects the framers' commitment to checks and balances even in crisis situations.

As American society becomes more complex and the presidency more demanding, the Twenty Fifth Amendment's importance may only grow. Its provisions continue to evolve through precedent and practice, demonstrating how constitutional amendments can provide both specific solutions to immediate problems and flexible frameworks for addressing future challenges.

Youth Vote: Twenty-Sixth Amendment Movement

The drive to lower the voting age to eighteen emerged from one of America's most turbulent periods, when thousands of young Americans were being drafted to fight in Vietnam while being denied the right to vote. The rallying cry "old enough to fight, old enough to vote" resonated across college campuses and city streets as young people demanded their voice in democracy.

The movement to lower the voting age had actually begun decades earlier during World War II, when President Franklin D. Roosevelt lowered the military draft age to eighteen. This discrepancy between the age of military service and voting rights created an obvious moral tension that would only grow more pronounced in the following decades. President Eisenhower, in his 1954 State of the Union address, became the first president to explicitly endorse lowering the voting age, arguing that if young people were mature enough to fight, they were mature enough to vote.

The Vietnam War transformed this long-simmering issue into an urgent demand for change. As the conflict escalated in the 1960s, the stark reality that eighteen-year-olds could be conscripted and sent to die in Southeast Asia while lacking any say in the political decisions that sent them there became increasingly untenable. Student activists and anti-war protesters made voting rights a central part of their broader critique of American society and the war effort.

The political momentum for change built slowly but steadily. By 1970, four states (Georgia, Kentucky, Alaska, and Hawaii) had already lowered their voting age to eighteen for state and local elections. Congress attempted to address the issue through legislation, passing provisions in the Voting Rights Act of 1970 that lowered the voting age to eighteen for all elections, state and federal. However, in Oregon v.

Mitchell (1970), the Supreme Court ruled that Congress could set the voting age for federal elections but lacked the power to regulate state and local voting ages through ordinary legislation.

This split decision created an administrative nightmare, with states potentially having to maintain separate voting rolls for federal and state elections. The prospect of this costly and confusing dual system helped build support for a constitutional amendment. Senator Jennings Randolph of West Virginia, who had been introducing voting age amendments since 1942, found his colleagues finally ready to act.

The amendment process moved with remarkable speed, reflecting broad bipartisan consensus on the need for change. The Senate voted 94-0 in favor, and the House approved it by a vote of 401-19. State ratification proceeded even more quickly than the recently approved Twenty Fifth Amendment, with the required thirty-eight states ratifying in just over two months. The Twenty Sixth Amendment became part of the Constitution on July 1, 1971, making it the fastest ratification in American history.

The amendment's text was straightforward: "The right of citizens of the United States, who are eighteen years of age or older, to vote shall not be denied or abridged by the United States or by any State on account of age." A second section gave Congress enforcement power through appropriate legislation. This simplicity helped speed its passage, as did the amendment's focus on a single issue rather than broader electoral reforms.

The immediate impact was substantial, with approximately 11 million new voters between eighteen and twenty-one becoming eligible to participate in the 1972 presidential election. Political parties and candidates scrambled to appeal to these new voters, developing youth outreach strategies and addressing issues of particular concern to young Americans. The 1972 election saw the first sustained effort to cultivate the "youth vote" as a distinct political force.

The amendment's passage represented more than just an expansion of voting rights; it marked a significant shift in American attitudes about youth, citizenship, and political participation. The idea that eighteen-year-olds were mature enough to exercise responsible political judgment reflected changing views about adolescence and young adulthood in American society.

Critics had long argued that eighteen-year-olds lacked the maturity and judgment necessary for voting, but supporters pointed to their military service, workforce participation, and civic engagement as evidence of their readiness for full citizenship rights. The amendment's ratification effectively settled this debate, establishing eighteen as the national standard for electoral majority.

The Twenty Sixth Amendment's legacy extends beyond its immediate impact on voting rights. It demonstrated how social movements could translate moral arguments into constitutional change, particularly when those arguments exposed contradictions in existing law. The amendment also showed how wartime circumstances could accelerate democratic reforms, as had happened previously with women's suffrage during World War I.

In subsequent decades, the amendment has sparked ongoing discussions about youth political participation and civic education. While eighteen remains the voting age, debates continue about how to engage young voters and whether the age should be lowered further for local elections. Some municipalities have experimented with allowing sixteen-year-olds to vote in local elections, drawing on similar arguments about youth civic capacity that helped pass the Twenty Sixth Amendment.

The amendment also raises broader questions about the relationship between military service and citizenship rights, a connection that dates back to the republic's founding. While the draft ended shortly after the amendment's ratification, the principle that civic obligations should be matched with civic rights remains powerful in American political thought.

Today, as youth political activism continues to shape American public life, from climate change to gun control, the Twenty Sixth Amendment stands as a reminder of young people's capacity to drive constitutional change. Its rapid ratification demonstrates how seemingly immovable barriers to participation can fall when moral arguments align with political necessity.

Congressional Pay: Twenty-Seventh's 200-Year Journey

The Twenty Seventh Amendment stands as perhaps the most unusual addition to the Constitution, taking an astounding 202 years and 7 months from its initial proposal to final ratification. This marathon journey from proposal to law began in 1789 when James Madison included it among the original twelve amendments he proposed to the First Congress, of which ten would become the Bill of Rights.

The amendment's text is deceptively simple: "No law, varying the compensation for the services of the Senators and Representatives shall take effect, until an election of Representatives shall have intervened." In other words, Congress cannot give itself an immediate pay raise; any salary increase they vote for themselves can only take effect after the next election, when voters have had a chance to hold them accountable.

Madison's original concern stemmed from the Constitution's requirement that Congress set its own pay. He worried this power could be abused, with legislators voting themselves ever-larger salaries without facing immediate consequences from their constituents. The amendment was meant to create a buffer between the vote for a pay raise and its implementation, ensuring voters would have a say in whether their representatives deserved the increase.

When first proposed, the amendment received relatively little attention compared to other items in Madison's package. By 1791, only six states had ratified it while eleven states were needed. The amendment then entered a prolonged period of dormancy, occasionally resurfacing when congressional pay became a contentious issue but never gaining significant momentum. For nearly two centuries, it seemed destined to remain in constitutional limbo.

The amendment's remarkable revival began in 1982 with an unlikely catalyst: a university sophomore's term paper. Gregory Watson, a student at the University of Texas at Austin, discovered the unratified amendment while researching a government class assignment. Intrigued by its relevance to modern concerns about congressional compensation, Watson began investigating whether the amendment could still be ratified. His professor was unimpressed, giving him a C on the paper and rejecting his argument that the amendment remained viable.

Undeterred, Watson launched a one-man campaign to achieve ratification. He wrote letters to state legislators across the country, arguing that the amendment had no deadline and could still become law. His timing proved fortunate, as public frustration with congressional pay raises was growing. In 1989, Congress had triggered particular outrage by voting itself a substantial salary increase while simultaneously making it harder for constituents to track their voting records on pay issues.

Watson's persistent advocacy began bearing fruit. Maine became the first state in the modern era to ratify the amendment in 1983, followed by Colorado in 1984. The pace accelerated as more state legislators became aware of the opportunity to respond to public anger over congressional compensation. The movement gained substantial momentum in the late 1980s, as public attention focused on congressional ethics and salary issues.

The question of whether such a long-delayed ratification could be valid sparked considerable debate among constitutional scholars. Some argued that amendments should be ratified within a "reasonable time," pointing to the Supreme Court's suggestion in Dillon v. Gloss (1921) that ratification should be sufficiently contemporaneous to reflect a current consensus. Others countered that since the original proposal included no time limit, unlike many modern amendments, there was no constitutional barrier to delayed ratification.

On May 7, 1992, Michigan became the 38th state to ratify the amendment, crossing the three-fourths threshold required for ratification. The Archivist of the United States certified the amendment on May 18, 1992, and Congress subsequently voted to accept the certification, though some argued this step wasn't constitutionally necessary.

The Twenty Seventh Amendment's ratification represents a remarkable instance of citizen initiative changing the Constitution. Gregory Watson's persistent advocacy demonstrated how a single determined individual could revive a long-dormant proposal and shepherd it to ratification. His success challenged conventional wisdom about the amendment process and showed that constitutional change could come from unexpected sources.

The amendment's practical impact has been somewhat limited, as Congress has found other ways to adjust its compensation, including automatic cost-of-living increases. However, its ratification story has become a powerful example of democratic persistence and the Constitution's adaptability. The fact that an amendment proposed by James Madison could be ratified in the age of computers and television demonstrates the founding generation's continuing relevance to modern governance.

The amendment's journey also raises important questions about constitutional time frames and the nature of consensus in a democratic society. Can an amendment truly reflect the will of "We the People" when ratification spans multiple generations? The answer seems to be yes, as evidenced by the contemporary support for the amendment's principles and Congress's willing acceptance of its ratification.

Today, the Twenty Seventh Amendment serves as both a practical constraint on congressional compensation and a testament to the democratic process's unpredictability. Its unique ratification story continues to inspire citizens who seek constitutional change, suggesting that patience, persistence, and principled advocacy can eventually overcome even the most formidable obstacles to reform.

Early Supreme Court: Defining Amendment Powers

In the early years of the American republic, the Supreme Court played a crucial role in defining how constitutional amendments would shape the nation's legal landscape. Under Chief Justice John Marshall's leadership from 1801 to 1835, the Court established fundamental principles about the scope and meaning of constitutional amendments that continue to influence jurisprudence today.

The Court's first major encounter with interpreting constitutional amendments came in Barron v. Baltimore (1833), where the justices had to determine whether the Bill of Rights applied to state governments. Chief Justice Marshall, writing for a unanimous court, established that the first ten amendments were intended solely as limitations on federal power, not state actions. This decision would have profound implications for American constitutional law, requiring later generations to use the Fourteenth Amendment to apply key rights to the states through the doctrine of incorporation.

The Marshall Court also grappled with the Eleventh Amendment's impact on federal court jurisdiction in cases involving states. In Cohens v. Virginia (1821), the Court had to balance state sovereignty with federal authority, ultimately determining that the Supreme Court could review state court decisions in criminal cases when they involved federal questions. This interpretation helped establish the delicate balance between state and federal power that would characterize American federalism.

Another significant early case was McCulloch v. Maryland (1819), which, while not directly interpreting an amendment, established principles that would prove crucial for understanding the scope of constitutional changes. Marshall's expansive reading of federal power under the Necessary and Proper Clause provided a framework for interpreting constitutional provisions broadly to achieve their intended purposes, a principle later applied to amendments.

The Court's approach to amendment interpretation evolved further under Chief Justice Roger Taney, who succeeded Marshall in 1836. In Luther v. Borden (1849), the Court confronted questions about how constitutional amendments affected the federal government's role in ensuring states maintained republican forms of government. The decision established the "political question" doctrine, suggesting some amendment-related issues might be beyond judicial review.

Perhaps the most significant early discussion of amendment powers came in the Court's handling of cases involving the Bill of Rights. In cases like United States v. Carpenter (1819) and Houston v. Moore (1820), the justices began developing frameworks for understanding how these fundamental rights should be interpreted and enforced. These early decisions established that while amendments could create new rights and powers, they needed to be understood within the broader constitutional structure.

The Court's early jurisprudence also addressed the relationship between different amendments. When confronted with potential conflicts between constitutional provisions, the justices developed principles for harmonizing various parts of the Constitution, including its amendments. This approach recognized that each amendment became an integral part of the Constitution, requiring interpretation that considered the document as a whole.

The justices of this era faced unique challenges in interpreting amendments because they often had direct knowledge of the founding period and the intended meaning of constitutional provisions. This personal connection to the Constitution's origins influenced their approach to amendment interpretation, sometimes leading them to rely heavily on their understanding of original intent.

The Court's early decisions also established important principles about the process of constitutional amendment itself. While Article V outlined the basic procedure for amending the Constitution, many questions remained about the details of this process. Through various cases and opinions, the Court helped clarify issues such as the role of state ratification, the timing of amendments, and the relationship between amendment proposals and other constitutional processes.

One particularly important principle established during this period was that amendments should be interpreted with sufficient flexibility to address changing circumstances while remaining true to their fundamental purposes. This balance between stability and adaptability would prove crucial as the nation faced new challenges and technologies unforeseen by the amendment's authors.

The early Supreme Court's handling of amendment powers also reflected the broader political and social context of the early republic. As the nation grappled with questions of federalism, individual rights, and national power, the Court's interpretations of constitutional amendments helped shape these debates and establish enduring principles of American law.

The justices recognized that amendments represented the highest expression of popular sovereignty under the Constitution. Their decisions therefore treated amendment interpretation with particular care, acknowledging that these provisions reflected the direct will of the people to modify their fundamental law.

The Court's early jurisprudence also established important precedents about the scope of judicial review in amendment-related cases. While maintaining the power to interpret amendments, the justices showed considerable deference to the political branches in implementing constitutional changes, recognizing that some aspects of amendment enforcement required political rather than judicial solutions.

These early decisions continue to influence modern constitutional law. The frameworks established for interpreting amendments, understanding their relationship to other constitutional provisions, and balancing competing rights and powers remain relevant to contemporary legal debates. The early Supreme Court's careful attention to amendment powers helped establish a foundation for constitutional interpretation that has proven remarkably durable over time.

Reconstruction's Impact: Post-Civil War Amendments

The period following the Civil War marked one of the most transformative eras in American constitutional history, as the nation grappled with fundamental questions about citizenship, equality, and federal power through three groundbreaking amendments. The Thirteenth, Fourteenth, and Fifteenth Amendments, collectively known as the Reconstruction Amendments, fundamentally reshaped American democracy and continue to influence constitutional law today.

The implementation of these amendments proved extraordinarily challenging in the face of southern resistance and northern fatigue. While the Thirteenth Amendment's prohibition of slavery met with relatively little legal opposition, southern states quickly moved to establish Black Codes that severely restricted the rights of newly freed African Americans. These restrictions prompted Congress to pass the Civil Rights Act of 1866 and ultimately led to the more comprehensive Fourteenth Amendment.

The Fourteenth Amendment's impact was immediately complicated by narrow judicial interpretations. The Supreme Court's decision in the Slaughterhouse Cases (1873) effectively gutted the Privileges or Immunities Clause, which many of the amendment's framers had intended as its primary enforcement mechanism. This decision forced civil rights advocates to rely more heavily on the Due Process and Equal Protection Clauses, fundamentally altering the amendment's early development.

Southern resistance to Reconstruction took many forms, from legal challenges to violent suppression of African American voting rights. The Ku Klux Klan and similar organizations terrorized black communities and their white allies, leading Congress to pass multiple enforcement acts under the new amendments. These laws represented the first significant expansion of federal power to protect individual rights against state and private action.

The Fifteenth Amendment's prohibition of racial discrimination in voting faced particularly fierce opposition. Southern states developed numerous techniques to disenfranchise African American voters while technically complying with the amendment's language. Poll taxes, literacy tests, and grandfather clauses created a web of restrictions that would take nearly a century to fully dismantle.

The Supreme Court's interpretation of the Reconstruction Amendments in the late nineteenth century generally favored a narrow reading that limited federal power to enforce civil rights. In United States v. Cruikshank (1876), the Court restricted the federal government's ability to prosecute private individuals for civil rights violations. The Civil Rights Cases (1883) further limited federal authority by striking down the Civil Rights Act of 1875 and establishing the "state action" doctrine that would long constrain civil rights enforcement.

Perhaps most infamously, Plessy v. Ferguson (1896) upheld racial segregation under the "separate but equal" doctrine, effectively blessing Jim Crow laws across the South. This decision represented a profound betrayal of the Reconstruction Amendments' promise of equality and citizenship, establishing a regime of legal discrimination that would persist until the mid-twentieth century.

The amendments' impact on federalism was equally profound. The Fourteenth Amendment in particular dramatically altered the balance between state and federal power, though this shift would not be fully realized until the twentieth century. The amendment's requirement that states respect fundamental rights and provide equal protection created a new framework for federal oversight of state actions.

The Reconstruction Amendments also transformed American citizenship. The Fourteenth Amendment's Citizenship Clause overturned the Dred Scott decision and established a national standard for citizenship based on birth in the United States. This revolutionary change would have lasting implications for immigration, naturalization, and the rights of various minority groups.

The economic implications of the Reconstruction Amendments proved surprisingly far-reaching. While initially focused on protecting civil rights, the Fourteenth Amendment's Due Process Clause became a powerful tool for protecting property rights and corporate interests. This development, though perhaps unintended by the amendment's framers, significantly influenced American economic development.

The amendments' impact on criminal justice was also significant. The Fourteenth Amendment's Due Process Clause eventually led to the incorporation of most Bill of Rights protections against state actions, fundamentally reshaping American criminal procedure. This process, though gradual, represented a profound shift in how constitutional rights were understood and enforced.

The legacy of the Reconstruction Amendments continues to evolve. Modern civil rights movements have repeatedly drawn on these amendments to advance causes their framers might never have imagined, from school desegregation to marriage equality. Their broad language about equality and citizenship rights has proven remarkably adaptable to changing social conditions.

The amendments' influence on constitutional theory has been equally lasting. They represented the first major attempt to use constitutional amendments to achieve social reform, establishing a pattern that later movements would follow. Their implementation challenges also highlighted the complex relationship between constitutional text, judicial interpretation, and social reality.

Today, debates about the meaning and scope of the Reconstruction Amendments remain central to American constitutional law. Questions about affirmative action, voting rights, and the proper balance between state and federal power continue to turn on interpretations of these transformative provisions. Their history reminds us that constitutional change, while powerful, requires sustained effort to translate legal principles into lived reality.

Progressive Era Reforms: Social Movement Success

The Progressive Era marked a transformative period in American constitutional history, as social movements successfully pushed through four constitutional amendments in just seven years. This unprecedented burst of constitutional change reflected the era's broader reform spirit and demonstrated the power of organized citizens to reshape their fundamental law.

The Sixteenth Amendment, ratified in 1913, fundamentally altered the federal government's financial powers by explicitly authorizing a federal income tax. This amendment emerged from decades of populist and progressive demands for a more equitable tax system. The Supreme Court's 1895 decision in Pollock v. Farmers' Loan & Trust Co. had struck down an earlier income tax law, making a constitutional amendment necessary. The successful ratification campaign united farmers, labor unions, and urban reformers who saw progressive taxation as essential for addressing the vast inequalities of the Gilded Age.

That same year, progressives achieved another major victory with the Seventeenth Amendment, which established direct election of United States Senators. Previously, senators had been chosen by state legislatures, a system that reformers criticized as prone to corruption and special interest influence. The amendment campaign gained momentum through widespread reports of bribery in senate selections and the growing power of popular democracy movements. State level reforms had already created various mechanisms for popular input into senate selection, but the amendment nationalized the principle of direct election.

The progressive movement's most controversial achievement came with the Eighteenth Amendment's establishment of national prohibition in 1919. Unlike other progressive reforms that expanded democratic participation, prohibition represented an attempt to impose social reform through constitutional mandate. The amendment's passage reflected the remarkable organizing power of the temperance movement, particularly the Woman's Christian Temperance Union and the Anti-Saloon League. These groups successfully framed alcohol as a source of social ills and corrupt political influence.

The era's constitutional reforms culminated in the Nineteenth Amendment's guarantee of women's suffrage in 1920. This victory represented the culmination of more than seventy years of organized activism by women's rights advocates. The suffrage movement had achieved significant state level victories, particularly in western states, before finally securing national constitutional change. The amendment campaign demonstrated sophisticated political organizing, combining traditional lobbying with new tactics like picketing the White House and hunger strikes.

These amendments shared several distinctive features that characterized Progressive Era reform. Each emerged from broad based social movements that combined moral reform impulses with democratic political goals. The amendments generally aimed to make American government more directly accountable to voters and less susceptible to corrupt influence. They also significantly expanded federal power to address social problems previously left to state regulation.

The success of these reforms reflected changes in how Americans approached constitutional amendment. Earlier amendments had largely focused on structural issues or civil rights guarantees. The Progressive Era amendments represented a new willingness to use constitutional change as a tool for social reform. This approach would influence later amendment campaigns throughout the twentieth century.

The implementation of these amendments varied significantly. The income tax and direct election of senators became permanent features of American government, though debates about tax policy continue. Prohibition proved unenforceable and was eventually repealed by the Twenty First Amendment, the only instance of one amendment explicitly overturning another. Women's suffrage dramatically expanded the electorate but did not immediately transform gender politics as some supporters had hoped.

The Progressive Era amendments also demonstrated the importance of state level reform efforts in building momentum for constitutional change. Each successful amendment campaign built on previous victories in state constitutions and laws. This pattern of state experimentation leading to national reform would become a common feature of American constitutional development.

The era's constitutional achievements inspired subsequent reform movements throughout the twentieth century. Labor unions, civil rights organizations, and other progressive groups sought to build on these successes with additional amendments. While few of these later efforts succeeded, they drew on the organizational techniques and reform philosophy developed during the Progressive Era.

The period's constitutional changes also significantly influenced judicial interpretation of federal power. The Supreme Court's understanding of congressional authority to regulate commerce and levy taxes evolved partly in response to these amendments. The era's reforms thus contributed to the growth of federal government capacity that would prove crucial during the New Deal and beyond.

These amendments reflected and reinforced the Progressive Era's faith in democracy and constitutional reform as solutions to social problems. While this faith would be tested by later developments, the period's constitutional achievements demonstrated the potential for organized citizens to fundamentally reshape their government through peaceful, legal change.

The legacies of Progressive Era amendments continue to influence contemporary debates about democratic reform, federal power, and social change through constitutional means. Their history offers important lessons about the relationship between social movements and constitutional change, the role of state level reform in building national momentum, and the challenges of implementing sweeping constitutional reforms.

Civil Rights and Amendments: The Long Struggle

The struggle for civil rights represents one of the most profound intersections between social movements and constitutional change in American history. While the Reconstruction Amendments laid the legal foundation for civil rights, turning these constitutional promises into reality required decades of sustained activism, legal battles, and further constitutional reform.

The civil rights movement's relationship with constitutional amendments reveals both the power and limitations of formal constitutional change. The Fourteenth and Fifteenth Amendments guaranteed equal protection and voting rights, but these protections were systematically undermined through Jim Crow laws, discriminatory practices, and outright violence. Southern states developed elaborate systems of disenfranchisement, including literacy tests, poll taxes, and white primaries, that effectively nullified constitutional voting rights.

The movement for racial equality pursued multiple strategies to overcome these barriers. Legal organizations like the NAACP focused on challenging discriminatory laws through constitutional litigation, gradually building precedents that would ultimately lead to landmark decisions like Brown v. Board of Education. Simultaneously, grassroots activists organized direct action campaigns that dramatized the gap between constitutional promises and lived reality.

Constitutional amendment emerged as a crucial tool in this struggle, particularly regarding voting rights. The Twenty Fourth Amendment, ratified in 1964, prohibited poll taxes in federal elections, eliminating one of the most persistent mechanisms of disenfranchisement. This amendment represented a direct response to civil rights movement demands and demonstrated how constitutional change could target specific tools of oppression.

The movement's influence extended beyond amendments explicitly focused on racial equality. The Twenty Third Amendment, giving District of Columbia residents the right to vote in presidential elections, partly reflected concerns about disenfranchisement of the district's largely African American population. Similarly, the Twenty Sixth Amendment's expansion of voting rights to eighteen year olds connected to broader demands for democratic participation.

Civil rights activists developed sophisticated strategies for pursuing constitutional change. They recognized that amendments alone were insufficient without robust enforcement mechanisms and public support. The movement therefore combined amendment advocacy with litigation, legislation, and mass mobilization. This comprehensive approach helped secure the Civil Rights Act of 1964 and Voting Rights Act of 1965, which gave practical effect to constitutional guarantees.

The relationship between civil rights and constitutional amendment also reveals important lessons about the timing and strategy of constitutional change. Successful amendments often came after years of movement building, legal precedents, and state level reforms had created favorable conditions. The Twenty Fourth Amendment, for instance, followed earlier state actions abolishing poll taxes and Supreme Court decisions limiting their use.

The civil rights movement's experience highlighted the importance of building broad coalitions for constitutional change. Successful amendment campaigns required support beyond the African American community, incorporating labor unions, religious groups, and other civil rights organizations. These coalitions helped overcome the significant hurdles of the amendment process, particularly in securing ratification from hostile state legislatures.

The movement's constitutional advocacy also extended beyond traditional civil rights issues. Economic justice emerged as a crucial concern, with activists arguing that meaningful constitutional equality required addressing poverty and economic discrimination. While proposals for amendments guaranteeing economic rights did not succeed, they influenced broader debates about the meaning of constitutional equality.

The civil rights struggle transformed understanding of existing amendments, particularly the Fourteenth Amendment's equal protection clause. Through litigation and public advocacy, the movement expanded constitutional protections to address various forms of discrimination. This evolution demonstrated how social movements could change constitutional meaning without formal amendment.

The period also saw important debates about the relationship between federal and state power in protecting civil rights. Amendments and enforcement legislation significantly expanded federal authority to protect constitutional rights, overcoming states' rights arguments that had long blocked civil rights progress. This shift represented a fundamental reorientation of American federalism.

The civil rights movement's constitutional legacy extends beyond specific amendments to include broader changes in constitutional culture. The movement established important precedents for how marginalized groups could use constitutional advocacy to advance their rights. Later movements for women's rights, LGBTQ equality, and disability rights drew on these experiences.

Implementation challenges remained even after successful constitutional changes. The movement continued fighting to protect and enforce constitutional rights against ongoing resistance. This experience highlighted the need for sustained activism even after formal constitutional change, a lesson that remains relevant for contemporary rights movements.

The civil rights struggle also influenced international constitutional development. American civil rights amendments and enforcement legislation provided models for other nations addressing discrimination and minority rights. The movement's nonviolent tactics and constitutional strategies inspired similar efforts globally.

Contemporary civil rights challenges demonstrate the ongoing relevance of this constitutional history. Debates over voting rights, police reform, and racial justice often center on constitutional questions first raised during the civil rights movement. Understanding this history remains crucial for current efforts to achieve constitutional equality.

The relationship between civil rights and constitutional amendment reveals both the potential and limitations of formal constitutional change in advancing equality. While amendments provided crucial tools for civil rights progress, their effectiveness ultimately depended on broader social and political transformation. This complex interplay between law and social change continues to shape American constitutional development.

States vs. Federal Power: Amendment Battles

The tension between state and federal power has been a defining feature of American constitutional development, particularly in the context of constitutional amendments. This fundamental conflict has shaped not only the substance of amendments but also the process of their adoption and implementation, creating a complex dance between national authority and state sovereignty.

From the earliest days of the republic, amendments have served as battlegrounds for competing visions of federalism. The Bill of Rights itself initially applied only to the federal government, reflecting a careful balance that preserved state autonomy. This arrangement would persist until the adoption of the Fourteenth Amendment and the subsequent development of the incorporation doctrine, which gradually applied most constitutional protections to the states.

The Civil War fundamentally altered this balance. The Reconstruction Amendments represented an unprecedented expansion of federal power, authorizing Congress to enforce civil rights protections against state violations. Southern states fiercely resisted these changes, leading to decades of conflict over the scope of federal enforcement authority. This resistance highlighted a persistent pattern: states often viewed constitutional amendments as potential threats to their sovereignty and autonomy.

The Progressive Era brought new dimensions to this conflict. The Sixteenth Amendment, authorizing a federal income tax, sparked intense debates about the proper scope of federal revenue powers. States worried that direct federal taxation would diminish their own revenue-raising capacity and create dangerous dependencies on federal funding. Similarly, the Seventeenth Amendment's provision for direct election of senators transformed a key structural protection for state interests in the federal system.

Prohibition exemplified the complexities of federal-state relations in constitutional change. The Eighteenth Amendment created a national ban on alcohol but relied heavily on state cooperation for enforcement. This arrangement proved problematic, as many states resisted dedicating resources to enforcement or actively undermined federal efforts. The Twenty First Amendment's repeal of Prohibition returned significant control over alcohol regulation to the states, demonstrating how constitutional amendments could both expand and contract federal authority.

The twentieth century saw increasing federal assertion of power through constitutional amendments, often in response to state practices deemed problematic. The Twenty Fourth Amendment's ban on poll taxes in federal elections directly targeted state voting restrictions. Similarly, the Twenty Sixth Amendment nationalized voting age requirements, overriding state variations. These changes reflected growing acceptance of federal authority to establish uniform national standards for fundamental rights.

State ratification battles have often become proxy wars over federalism principles. States frequently delayed or rejected amendments they viewed as excessive federal intrusions. The Equal Rights Amendment's failure to achieve ratification partly reflected state concerns about federal oversight of gender relations. Even the Twenty Seventh Amendment's two-century ratification process involved ongoing debates about federal versus state authority over congressional compensation.

Court interpretations have played a crucial role in mediating these conflicts. Supreme Court decisions have repeatedly addressed the scope of congressional enforcement powers under various amendments, particularly the Reconstruction Amendments. These rulings have sometimes expanded and sometimes contracted federal authority, reflecting the judiciary's own evolving views on federalism.

Modern debates continue to center on state-federal tensions in constitutional change. Proposed amendments often face opposition based on federalism concerns, whether they address balanced budget requirements, term limits, or campaign finance. States remain vigilant against perceived federal overreach through constitutional amendment, while reform advocates argue that national solutions are necessary for certain problems.

The development of cooperative federalism has somewhat modified these dynamics. Many modern constitutional provisions operate through federal-state partnerships rather than strict hierarchical arrangements. This approach recognizes the practical necessity of state cooperation while maintaining federal constitutional supremacy.

State constitutions have also evolved in response to federal constitutional changes, sometimes providing greater protections or different approaches to similar issues. This interplay between state and federal constitutional development has created a rich dialogue about rights and governmental authority in the American federal system.

The amendment process itself embodies federal-state tension, requiring both national consensus through congressional proposal and state-by-state ratification. This mechanism ensures that constitutional changes must navigate both national and state interests, often leading to compromises that respect both levels of authority.

Implementation challenges frequently reveal the practical dimensions of state-federal conflicts over amendments. States may resist through passive non-compliance, inadequate enforcement resources, or legal challenges to federal implementation measures. These dynamics have influenced how amendments actually function in practice, sometimes limiting their effective scope.

The experience of constitutional amendments in American federalism suggests several enduring patterns. Successful amendments often require careful attention to state concerns and interests. They frequently emerge from extended periods of state-level experimentation and consensus building. And their ultimate effectiveness depends significantly on state cooperation and support.

Looking forward, questions of state versus federal authority continue to shape debates about potential constitutional changes. Whether addressing voting rights, campaign finance, or other issues, proposed amendments must navigate persistent tensions between national standards and state autonomy. Understanding this historical dynamic remains crucial for future efforts at constitutional change.

Failed Amendments: What Could Have Been

The story of failed constitutional amendments reveals as much about American democracy as the successful ones. For every change that made it into our Constitution, many more proposals fell short, each representing paths not taken in our nation's development.

Perhaps the most notable near miss was the Equal Rights Amendment (ERA), which came tantalizingly close to ratification in the 1970s. The ERA's simple declaration that "Equality of rights under the law shall not be denied or abridged by the United States or by any State on account of sex" garnered widespread initial support. After passing Congress in 1972, it quickly secured 35 of the needed 38 state ratifications. However, a powerful conservative backlash led by Phyllis Schlafly raised concerns about draft requirements for women and traditional family structures, ultimately stalling the amendment's momentum. Despite recent renewed interest and symbolic ratifications, the ERA remains in constitutional limbo.

The Child Labor Amendment of 1924 represents another significant failure. Proposed in response to widespread exploitation of children in factories and mines, it would have given Congress power to regulate or prohibit labor of persons under eighteen. While the amendment passed Congress with strong support, it faced fierce opposition from business interests and states' rights advocates. Only 28 states ratified it, though its goals were largely achieved through later legislation and court decisions.

Several proposed amendments have sought to address the thorny issue of school prayer. Following the Supreme Court's decisions prohibiting mandatory prayer in public schools, numerous amendments were introduced to permit or restore religious exercises in schools. Despite significant popular support, none achieved the necessary congressional supermajority, reflecting deep divisions over church-state separation.

The balanced budget amendment has been a perennial proposal since the 1970s. Requiring federal spending to match revenues except in specific circumstances, it has come close to passage several times. In 1995, it fell just one vote short in the Senate. Supporters argue it would force fiscal responsibility, while opponents warn it would hamstring government response to economic crises.

Some failed amendments reflected immediate political controversies. After the disputed 1876 presidential election, proposals emerged to eliminate the Electoral College in favor of direct popular vote. Similar efforts followed the 2000 and 2016 elections, when winners lost the popular vote, but none gained sufficient traction. The difficulty of changing such a fundamental aspect of the political system, combined with small states' reluctance to surrender their disproportionate influence, has repeatedly doomed these efforts.

Marriage-related amendments have also sparked intense debate. In response to state court decisions allowing same-sex marriage, proposals to constitutionally define marriage as between one man and one woman gained momentum in the early 2000s. The Federal Marriage Amendment came to votes in Congress but failed to achieve the required supermajority. These efforts became moot after the Supreme Court recognized same-sex marriage rights in 2015.

The history of failed amendments includes some remarkably specific proposals. In 1876, an amendment was proposed to abolish the presidency and replace it with an executive council. Another would have renamed the country "The United States of Earth." While these may seem amusing today, they reflect genuine attempts to reshape fundamental aspects of American governance.

Some failed amendments aimed to expand individual rights. A proposal to explicitly recognize environmental rights gained attention in the 1970s but never reached a congressional vote. Another would have guaranteed healthcare as a constitutional right. These reflect ongoing debates about which fundamental rights deserve constitutional protection.

The difficulty of amending the Constitution has led to creative attempts to circumvent the process. The National Popular Vote Interstate Compact, for instance, seeks to effectively eliminate the Electoral College through state-level agreements rather than constitutional amendment. Such efforts acknowledge the practical challenges of formal amendment while seeking alternative paths to reform.

Several amendments have sought to address specific Supreme Court decisions. Following the Court's campaign finance rulings, particularly Citizens United, numerous proposals emerged to explicitly authorize campaign spending restrictions. Others targeted decisions about property rights, criminal procedure, and other controversial areas. These attempts to overturn judicial interpretations through constitutional amendment have consistently fallen short.

The fate of failed amendments often reflects broader social and political dynamics. Some proposals were ahead of their time, addressing issues that would later be resolved through other means. Others represented temporary reactions to specific events or decisions that lost urgency as circumstances changed. Many failed simply because they could not generate the broad consensus required for constitutional change.

Constitutional scholars debate whether the difficulty of amendment serves a valuable purpose or unnecessarily constrains democratic evolution. The high failure rate of proposed amendments suggests the process works as designed, preventing hasty or inadequately supported changes. However, it may also indicate structural barriers to necessary reforms.

Failed amendments continue to influence constitutional development even in defeat. They often spark public debate, shape legislative alternatives, and influence judicial interpretation. The ERA, though unratified, has inspired significant legislation and judicial decisions advancing gender equality. Similarly, balanced budget amendment proposals have influenced fiscal policy discussions even without formal adoption.

Looking at failed amendments helps us understand the boundaries of constitutional change in America. They demonstrate both the aspirations and limitations of using formal amendment to address social and political challenges. Their stories remind us that constitutional development occurs not only through successful amendments but also through the ongoing dialogue about what changes are necessary and achievable in our constitutional system.

Amendment Processes: How Change Happens

The process of amending the United States Constitution reflects a delicate balance between stability and adaptability. While the Founders created a mechanism for constitutional change, they deliberately made it challenging, requiring broad consensus across different levels of government and among the American people.

Article V of the Constitution outlines two distinct paths for amendment. The first and only method used successfully thus far begins with Congress, where a proposed amendment must secure two-thirds approval in both chambers. The second method, never successfully employed, allows two-thirds of state legislatures to call for a constitutional convention. This untested path remains a subject of scholarly debate, with questions about how such a convention would operate and whether its scope could be limited.

Once proposed, amendments face an even greater hurdle: ratification by three-fourths of the states. This requirement has proven to be the graveyard of many amendment proposals, as securing agreement among such a large proportion of states demands extraordinary consensus. States may ratify through their legislatures or through state conventions, though the convention method has been used only once, for the Twenty-first Amendment repealing Prohibition.

The timeline for ratification has evolved through practice and judicial interpretation. Initially, the Constitution specified no time limit for ratification. This led to the unusual case of the Twenty-seventh Amendment, which was proposed in 1789 but not ratified until 1992. Following this experience, Congress began including ratification deadlines in amendment proposals, typically seven years, though this period can be extended as demonstrated during the push for the Equal Rights Amendment.

Social movements have historically played a crucial role in driving the amendment process. Successful amendments typically emerge from sustained grassroots efforts that build popular support and political pressure over time. The women's suffrage movement, for instance, spent decades organizing, protesting, and lobbying before securing the Nineteenth Amendment. Similarly, the civil rights movement's persistent efforts contributed to the passage of voting rights amendments.

The state ratification process involves complex political dynamics. State legislatures must navigate local politics, regional interests, and national pressures. Some states race to be among the first to ratify, while others deliberately delay to maximize their influence. The order of ratification can create momentum or signal resistance, influencing other states' decisions. The Tennessee legislature's dramatic ratification of the Nineteenth Amendment, secured by a single vote change, exemplifies the high stakes of these state-level battles.

Technical aspects of the amendment process have generated significant legal questions. Courts have addressed issues such as whether states can rescind their ratification votes before an amendment is fully ratified, the validity of ratification deadlines, and the role of state governors in the process. The Supreme Court has generally treated these as political questions, deferring to Congress's authority to determine when an amendment has been properly ratified.

The amendment process also involves crucial procedural decisions within Congress. The choice between joint resolution and bill format, the specific language of the proposal, and the inclusion of implementation provisions can significantly affect an amendment's chances of success. Congressional debates often focus as much on these technical aspects as on the substance of the proposed change.

Public education and media coverage play vital roles in the amendment process. Successful amendments typically require extensive public campaigns to explain their necessity and impact. The repeal of Prohibition, for instance, succeeded partly because advocates effectively communicated the amendment's failures and the benefits of repeal. Modern amendment efforts increasingly utilize social media and digital organizing tools to build support and counter opposition.

Interest groups and political organizations often emerge specifically to promote or oppose proposed amendments. These organizations develop sophisticated strategies combining lobbying, public relations, and grassroots mobilization. The fight over the Equal Rights Amendment saw the creation of competing organizations that fundamentally shaped the national debate and ultimately influenced the amendment's fate.

State-level political dynamics can significantly impact the amendment process. In some cases, state constitutional provisions or legislative rules create additional hurdles to ratification. The requirement in some states for supermajority votes or the influence of legislative committees can effectively block ratification even when popular support exists.

The amendment process also reflects broader changes in American political culture. Early amendments frequently focused on governmental structure and individual rights against federal power. Progressive Era amendments addressed social and economic issues, while later amendments increasingly dealt with voting rights and democratic participation. This evolution reflects changing conceptions of the Constitution's role in American society.

International influences have occasionally shaped amendment efforts. The Prohibition movement drew inspiration from similar efforts in other countries, while civil rights amendments were partly motivated by Cold War competition and international criticism of American racial practices. Modern amendment proposals often reference international human rights standards and comparative constitutional provisions.

The difficulty of the amendment process has led to alternative methods of constitutional change, including judicial interpretation, legislation, and executive action. However, formal amendments remain uniquely powerful in their ability to permanently alter the constitutional text and definitively settle certain questions of fundamental law.

Understanding how constitutional change happens requires recognizing the complex interplay between formal procedures and political reality. Successful amendments combine compelling substantive arguments with effective political organization, careful attention to procedural requirements, and the ability to build and maintain broad coalitions across regional and partisan lines.

Social Movements: Driving Constitutional Change

Throughout American history, social movements have been the driving force behind constitutional amendments, transforming public consciousness and political will into fundamental legal change. These movements, often starting with small groups of dedicated reformers, gradually built the massive coalitions necessary to achieve the supermajorities required for constitutional amendment.

The abolitionist movement provides one of the earliest and most powerful examples of how social movements can reshape the Constitution. Beginning with small religious and moral reform societies in the early 19th century, abolitionists gradually built a powerful movement that transformed public opinion in the North. While the Civil War ultimately proved necessary to end slavery, the groundwork laid by decades of abolitionist activism made the Thirteenth Amendment possible and helped shape the Fourteenth and Fifteenth Amendments that followed.

The women's suffrage movement demonstrated the importance of sustained organizing and strategic evolution in achieving constitutional change. Starting with the Seneca Falls Convention in 1848, suffragists spent over seventy years building their movement. They developed sophisticated political strategies, from constitutional test cases to massive street demonstrations. The movement's eventual success with the Nineteenth Amendment came only after decades of state-level victories and the development of new tactics like Alice Paul's militant suffragism.

The Progressive Era saw multiple social movements successfully push for constitutional change. The movement for direct election of senators, culminating in the Seventeenth Amendment, combined populist grassroots organizing with sophisticated political maneuvering. The income tax movement, leading to the Sixteenth Amendment, united farmers' alliances, labor unions, and urban reformers. Even the ultimately unsuccessful Prohibition movement demonstrated how determined activists could achieve constitutional change through sustained organizing and coalition building.

Civil rights movements of the mid-twentieth century showed how social movements could use multiple strategies to achieve constitutional change. While direct action and legal strategies were crucial, the movement also built political power that helped secure the Twenty-fourth Amendment banning poll taxes and influenced interpretation of earlier amendments, particularly the Fourteenth. The movement demonstrated how social movements could work simultaneously through multiple channels, from street protests to Supreme Court litigation to legislative lobbying.

The youth rights movement of the 1960s and early 1970s showed how rapidly social movements could sometimes achieve constitutional change. Building on the energy of anti-war protests and civil rights activism, young activists successfully argued that if eighteen-year-olds could be drafted to fight, they deserved the right to vote. The Twenty-sixth Amendment, lowering the voting age to eighteen, was ratified in just 100 days, the fastest ratification in American history.

Environmental movements, while not yet successful in achieving constitutional amendments, have demonstrated how social movements can reshape constitutional interpretation and build momentum for potential future amendments. Environmental activists have influenced interpretations of existing amendments and built support for proposals like the Green Amendment, showing how movements can work toward constitutional change even before achieving formal amendments.

Modern social movements have developed new strategies for pursuing constitutional change, adapting to technological and social transformations. Digital organizing tools allow movements to build support and coordinate action more rapidly than ever before. Social media enables quick dissemination of information and rapid mobilization of supporters. However, these same tools can also amplify opposition and create echo chambers that make building broad consensus more challenging.

The relationship between social movements and constitutional change often involves complex feedback loops. Movements may begin by seeking legislative change or court decisions, only turning to constitutional amendments when other approaches prove insufficient. Conversely, the difficulty of achieving amendments often pushes movements to seek alternative paths to their goals, through legislation, litigation, or state-level action.

Social movements pursuing constitutional change must balance multiple challenges. They need to maintain activist energy over the long periods typically required for amendment campaigns while also building broad coalitions that can secure supermajority support. They must frame their issues in ways that resonate with diverse audiences while remaining true to their core principles. They must work simultaneously at federal and state levels, often maintaining momentum through incremental victories while pursuing ultimate constitutional change.

The role of counter-movements has become increasingly important in constitutional politics. Movements seeking amendments often face organized opposition that can marshal its own grassroots support and political influence. The Equal Rights Amendment's defeat demonstrated how counter-movements could effectively block constitutional changes even after they had secured congressional approval and significant state support.

Modern movements for constitutional change increasingly recognize the need to build diverse coalitions across traditional political and social divisions. Successful movements typically combine grassroots activism with support from established institutions, unite urban and rural constituencies, and bridge partisan divides. They must also navigate the complex interaction between state and federal politics, often building momentum through state-level victories while working toward federal constitutional change.

The history of social movements and constitutional change reveals certain consistent patterns. Successful movements typically combine moral argumentation with practical political organization, build broad coalitions while maintaining activist energy, and work simultaneously through multiple channels of change. They often achieve significant social and legal changes even when falling short of their ultimate goal of constitutional amendment, demonstrating how the pursuit of amendments can catalyze broader social transformation.

State Ratification: The Final Steps

The path from a proposed constitutional amendment to its final ratification involves a complex series of steps that have shaped American democracy in profound ways. While the basic process outlined in Article V of the Constitution seems straightforward, the actual journey of amendments through state legislatures reveals the intricate dance between federal and state power that defines American federalism.

The constitutional requirement that three-fourths of states must ratify an amendment has created fascinating dynamics throughout American history. This high threshold ensures that amendments truly represent a broad national consensus rather than temporary or regional preferences. The founders deliberately made the process difficult, believing that constitutional changes should require overwhelming support from both the federal government and the states.

State ratification debates have often become intense battlegrounds where national issues meet local politics. During the ratification of the Bill of Rights, state legislatures engaged in heated discussions about the proper balance between federal and state power. Some states initially rejected certain amendments while approving others, leading to complex political negotiations. Massachusetts, for instance, didn't ratify the first ten amendments until 1939, long after they had become fundamental to American law.

The ratification process for the Fourteenth Amendment highlighted how political circumstances can dramatically affect state decisions. Southern states initially rejected the amendment, leading Congress to require its ratification as a condition for readmission to the Union after the Civil War. This controversial approach raised questions about the voluntary nature of state ratification that continue to influence constitutional debates today.

Time limits on ratification emerged as a crucial issue during the Progressive Era. The Eighteenth Amendment introducing Prohibition included a seven-year ratification deadline, establishing a precedent that would affect many subsequent amendments. This time limit concept became particularly significant during the extended ratification process of the Equal Rights Amendment, which failed to achieve ratification within its original seven-year period and a subsequent extension.

The Twenty-seventh Amendment's extraordinary ratification story demonstrates the potential complexity of the process. Originally proposed in 1789 as part of the Bill of Rights, this amendment regarding congressional pay raises wasn't ratified until 1992, more than two centuries later. This unprecedented gap between proposal and ratification raised new questions about time limits and the continuing validity of proposed amendments.

State ratification procedures vary significantly, adding another layer of complexity to the process. While most states use legislative votes, some have experimented with different approaches. Some states have considered using popular referendums for amendment ratification, though the constitutionality of this approach remains debated. The variation in state procedures reflects the federal system's respect for state autonomy in managing their internal processes.

The order of state ratifications often creates interesting political dynamics. Early ratifications can build momentum for an amendment, while early rejections can effectively kill it. States sometimes compete to be the decisive thirty-eighth state to ratify an amendment, seeking their place in constitutional history. This competition was particularly evident during the ratification of the Twenty-sixth Amendment lowering the voting age to eighteen.

Modern communication technology has transformed how states approach ratification. While early amendments saw states acting with limited knowledge of other states' decisions, today's instant communication allows for coordinated strategies and real-time responses to other states' actions. Social media and digital organizing have also increased public engagement in state ratification debates.

The role of state legislatures in the ratification process has evolved significantly. Early in American history, state legislators often saw themselves as independent actors in constitutional development. Modern state legislators typically align more closely with national party positions, though local interests and constituent pressures still influence their decisions on amendments.

Rescission attempts have added another layer of complexity to state ratification. Several states have attempted to rescind their previous ratifications of amendments, raising constitutional questions about whether states can reverse their ratification decisions before an amendment reaches the three-fourths threshold. This issue became particularly contentious during the ERA ratification process.

The interaction between state and federal courts during ratification has also shaped the process. State courts sometimes become involved in procedural questions about ratification votes, while federal courts have generally avoided intervening in state ratification processes, viewing them as political questions beyond judicial review.

Public engagement in state ratification debates has varied significantly across amendments and eras. While some amendments generated intense public interest and debate at the state level, others were ratified with relatively little public attention. Modern amendments typically involve sophisticated campaigns to influence state legislators, combining grassroots activism with professional lobbying.

The state ratification process remains a crucial safeguard ensuring that constitutional changes truly reflect national consensus. While some critics argue that the high threshold for state ratification makes necessary changes too difficult, supporters maintain that this deliberate process protects constitutional stability while allowing for meaningful change when truly broad support exists.

International Influence: Global Impact

The American Constitution has served as a model and inspiration for democratic governments worldwide since its creation, though its influence has evolved significantly over time. The document's blend of enumerated rights, separation of powers, and federalism created a template that many nations would study and adapt to their own circumstances.

In the immediate aftermath of American independence, the Constitution's influence was most strongly felt in Latin America. As Spanish colonies sought independence in the early 19th century, many looked to the United States Constitution as a blueprint. Nations like Argentina and Mexico adopted similar federal systems and bills of rights, though often with modifications reflecting their unique cultural and political circumstances.

The impact of American constitutional amendments has been particularly significant. The Bill of Rights, especially the First Amendment's protections of speech, religion, and assembly, has influenced human rights declarations and constitutions globally. When the United Nations drafted the Universal Declaration of Human Rights in 1948, the American Bill of Rights served as a key reference point, though the UN declaration ultimately went further in recognizing positive social and economic rights.

The Reconstruction Amendments profoundly shaped international human rights law and constitutional development. The Thirteenth Amendment's abolition of slavery influenced similar provisions worldwide and helped establish the principle that certain human rights are universal and non-derogable. The Fourteenth Amendment's concepts of due process and equal protection have been adapted by numerous countries, though often with broader interpretations than U.S. courts have given them.

Women's suffrage movements worldwide drew inspiration from the campaign for the Nineteenth Amendment. Activists in Britain, New Zealand, and other nations studied American suffragists' strategies and constitutional arguments. The amendment's eventual success helped build momentum for women's voting rights globally, though several countries actually preceded the United States in granting women's suffrage.

The influence hasn't been one-directional, however. American constitutional amendments have also been shaped by international developments. The Progressive Era amendments, including direct election of senators and income tax, were influenced by similar reforms in other democracies. More recently, international human rights law has influenced interpretations of constitutional amendments, particularly regarding cruel and unusual punishment under the Eighth Amendment.

Some nations have explicitly rejected certain aspects of the American constitutional model. Many modern democracies have opted for parliamentary systems rather than presidential ones, viewing the American separation of powers as potentially leading to gridlock. The Second Amendment's protection of individual gun rights remains uniquely American, with few other nations constitutionally protecting private firearm ownership.

The process of amending the U.S. Constitution has also influenced constitutional design globally. Some nations have adopted similar supermajority requirements for constitutional changes, while others have chosen more flexible amendment procedures. The debate over whether constitutions should be difficult or easy to amend remains active in constitutional design worldwide.

American constitutional jurisprudence, particularly Supreme Court interpretations of amendments, has significantly influenced courts worldwide. Citations to American constitutional cases appear in decisions from high courts across the globe, though this influence has somewhat declined in recent decades as other nations develop their own constitutional traditions.

The export of American constitutional ideas has often occurred through legal education. Foreign lawyers and judges studying in American law schools have carried constitutional concepts back to their home countries. American constitutional scholars have also advised numerous nations on constitutional design, though this influence has sometimes been criticized as legal imperialism.

The digital age has transformed how constitutional ideas spread globally. Online access to constitutional texts, court decisions, and scholarly analysis has accelerated the exchange of constitutional concepts. Social media allows activists worldwide to share strategies for constitutional change and rights protection.

International organizations have played a crucial role in spreading American constitutional principles while also critiquing American practices. The Venice Commission of the Council of Europe, for instance, regularly reviews constitutional changes worldwide, often referencing American experience while also pointing out where American practice falls short of international standards.

Modern constitution-makers often view the U.S. Constitution as both inspiration and cautionary tale. While admiring its durability and fundamental principles, they frequently seek to avoid what they see as its shortcomings, such as the electoral college or the difficulty of amendment. This has led to hybrid systems that combine American elements with other constitutional traditions.

The influence of American constitutional amendments continues to evolve in the 21st century. While the basic principles they represent remain influential, their specific implementations are increasingly viewed as one approach among many to protecting rights and structuring government. The global conversation about constitutionalism now involves a much broader range of voices and models.

Modern Interpretations: Living Constitution

The concept of a "living Constitution" has been one of the most contentious and influential ideas in American constitutional law. This approach to constitutional interpretation holds that the meaning of the Constitution's text, including its amendments, should evolve to meet the needs and values of contemporary society rather than remaining fixed in the understanding of those who originally ratified it.

Modern interpretations of constitutional amendments reflect this ongoing tension between originalist and living Constitution approaches. The Supreme Court's jurisprudence has increasingly acknowledged that many constitutional provisions must be understood in light of modern circumstances, even while attempting to remain faithful to core constitutional principles.

The First Amendment's protections, for instance, have been extended far beyond what its framers could have envisioned. Courts now grapple with questions of free speech in digital spaces, commercial advertising, and campaign finance – issues that would have been unimaginable in the 18th century. The notion that money constitutes speech, established in Buckley v. Valeo and expanded in Citizens United, represents a thoroughly modern interpretation of First Amendment principles.

Fourth Amendment jurisprudence has perhaps undergone the most dramatic modern reinterpretation. What began as a protection against physical intrusion into homes and papers now encompasses electronic surveillance, thermal imaging, GPS tracking, and cell phone data. The Supreme Court's decision in Carpenter v. United States, protecting cell phone location data, demonstrates how modern interpretations must balance traditional Fourth Amendment principles with technological reality.

The Fourteenth Amendment's equal protection clause has been particularly transformed by modern interpretation. While its original purpose was to protect newly freed slaves, courts have expanded its reach to address discrimination based on gender, sexual orientation, and other characteristics. The Supreme Court's decisions in cases like Obergefell v. Hodges, recognizing same-sex marriage rights, represent a dramatic evolution in constitutional understanding.

Modern interpretations have also grappled with the Second Amendment's application to contemporary weapons and circumstances. The Court's decisions in District of Columbia v. Heller and McDonald v. Chicago established an individual right to bear arms while acknowledging that this right, like others, is not unlimited. The ongoing debate over assault weapons and gun control measures reflects the challenge of applying 18th-century concepts to 21st-century realities.

The Eighth Amendment's prohibition on cruel and unusual punishment has been significantly reshaped by evolving standards of decency. Courts now consider international norms, scientific research, and changing social attitudes when determining what constitutes cruel and unusual punishment. Decisions limiting the death penalty's application and considering prison conditions reflect this dynamic approach.

Even seemingly straightforward provisions have required modern reinterpretation. The Twenty-Fifth Amendment's provisions for presidential succession and disability have taken on new importance in an era of nuclear weapons and instant communication. Scholars and officials debate how its provisions might apply to various scenarios involving presidential incapacity or inability to discharge duties.

The Commerce Clause, while not an amendment, demonstrates how constitutional interpretation has evolved to meet modern economic realities. From the interstate highway system to the internet, courts have had to adapt constitutional principles to an increasingly interconnected economy.

Modern interpretation has also emphasized the interrelationship between different amendments. Privacy rights, for instance, emerge from the interaction of several amendments, including the First, Fourth, and Fourteenth. This holistic approach to constitutional interpretation reflects the complexity of modern legal challenges.

Critics of the living Constitution approach argue that it undermines the stability and predictability of constitutional law, allowing judges to substitute their own preferences for the Constitution's fixed meaning. They contend that changes should come through the amendment process rather than judicial interpretation.

Defenders respond that rigid adherence to original understanding would render the Constitution ineffective in addressing modern challenges. They argue that the framers themselves understood that future generations would need to apply constitutional principles to new circumstances.

The debate over modern constitutional interpretation reflects broader questions about democracy, change, and continuity. How can a document written in the 18th century effectively govern a 21st-century society? How should courts balance fidelity to constitutional text with the need to address modern challenges?

Recent Supreme Court decisions have increasingly highlighted these interpretive tensions. Cases involving digital privacy, corporate speech rights, and government surveillance demonstrate the ongoing challenge of applying constitutional principles to modern circumstances.

The future of constitutional interpretation will likely continue to reflect this dynamic tension between original meaning and contemporary application. As technology advances and society evolves, courts will face new challenges in interpreting constitutional amendments in ways that preserve their fundamental principles while addressing modern realities.

Digital Age Rights: Amendments in Modern Times

The digital age has brought unprecedented challenges to constitutional rights and protections, forcing courts, legislators, and citizens to grapple with how traditional constitutional guarantees apply in an interconnected world. The rapid pace of technological change has created novel questions about privacy, speech, security, and equality that the framers of our constitutional amendments could never have anticipated.

Digital privacy has emerged as one of the most pressing constitutional concerns of our era. The vast amount of personal data generated by our online activities, smart devices, and digital communications has created new vulnerabilities that traditional Fourth Amendment protections struggle to address. While the Supreme Court's landmark decision in Carpenter v. United States extended Fourth Amendment protections to cell phone location data, many questions remain about the scope of constitutional privacy rights in the digital realm.

Social media platforms have become the new public square, raising complex questions about First Amendment rights in private digital spaces. When companies like Facebook or Twitter moderate content or ban users, they act as powerful gatekeepers of public discourse, yet traditional First Amendment protections only limit government action. This has led to calls for new constitutional frameworks to protect free expression in the digital age.

The rise of artificial intelligence and automated decision making systems has created novel equal protection concerns. When algorithms used in criminal sentencing, loan applications, or hiring decisions produce biased outcomes, they challenge traditional Fourteenth Amendment analysis. Courts must now consider whether algorithmic discrimination constitutes a constitutional violation, even when no human actor intended to discriminate.

Digital surveillance technologies have strained traditional Fourth Amendment doctrines. From facial recognition systems to predictive policing algorithms, law enforcement agencies now have unprecedented capabilities to monitor and track citizens. The constitutional standard of "reasonable expectation of privacy" established in Katz v. United States must be reconsidered in an era where privacy expectations are constantly evolving.

The Second Amendment has faced new questions in the digital age as well. The emergence of 3D printed firearms and online distribution of weapon designs has challenged traditional approaches to gun regulation. Courts must now consider whether sharing digital firearms blueprints constitutes protected speech or falls outside Second Amendment protections.

Electronic voting systems have raised new concerns about election integrity and the right to vote. While amendments like the Fifteenth, Nineteenth, and Twenty-sixth protect voting rights from discrimination, they provide little guidance on securing digital voting systems from tampering or ensuring equal access to electronic voting methods.

The global nature of the internet has complicated questions of jurisdiction and constitutional rights. When online speech crosses national borders or digital evidence exists on foreign servers, courts must balance constitutional protections with international law and sovereignty concerns. The traditional territorial limits of constitutional rights have become increasingly difficult to define in cyberspace.

Digital currencies and blockchain technology have raised novel questions about Congress's power to regulate commerce and currency under Article I and the Sixteenth Amendment's taxation provisions. The decentralized nature of these technologies challenges traditional assumptions about governmental authority over financial transactions.

The rise of remote work and digital communications has even affected interpretation of lesser known amendments. The Third Amendment's prohibition on quartering soldiers in private homes takes on new meaning when government surveillance can effectively occupy our digital homes. The Seventh Amendment's guarantee of jury trials must be reconsidered as courts experiment with remote proceedings and digital evidence presentation.

Privacy rights in the digital age often involve the interaction of multiple amendments. The First Amendment's protection of anonymous speech, the Fourth Amendment's privacy guarantees, and the Fifth Amendment's protection against self incrimination all come into play when considering government access to encrypted communications or online anonymity rights.

The speed of technological change has highlighted the challenge of applying constitutional principles to unforeseen circumstances. While the amendment process itself remains unchanged, the need for constitutional adaptation has never been more pressing. Some scholars argue for new amendments specifically addressing digital rights, while others advocate for flexible interpretation of existing provisions.

State constitutions have often moved more quickly than federal law in addressing digital rights. Several states have amended their constitutions to explicitly protect electronic privacy or digital access rights, potentially providing models for federal constitutional evolution.

The digital divide has created new equal protection challenges, as access to technology becomes increasingly essential for exercising constitutional rights. Courts must consider whether the government has an obligation to ensure equal access to digital resources when they become necessary for participating in democracy or accessing government services.

Looking ahead, emerging technologies like virtual reality, brain computer interfaces, and quantum computing will likely present even more novel constitutional questions. The challenge will be maintaining the fundamental principles of individual rights and limited government while adapting to technological realities the framers could never have imagined.

This ongoing evolution of constitutional rights in the digital age demonstrates both the resilience and limitations of our constitutional framework. While core principles of liberty, privacy, and equality remain relevant, their application must continually evolve to meet new challenges. The digital age may ultimately require us to fundamentally rethink how we conceptualize and protect constitutional rights in an increasingly virtual world.

First Amendment Online: New Frontiers

The emergence of social media platforms and digital communication technologies has fundamentally reshaped how Americans exercise their First Amendment rights. While the amendment's core protections of free speech, press, assembly, and religion remain unchanged, their application in the online sphere has created unprecedented legal and social challenges that continue to reshape our understanding of these fundamental freedoms.

Social media platforms have become the modern public square, hosting political debates, social movements, and daily discourse among millions of Americans. Yet unlike traditional public forums, these spaces are privately owned and operated, creating tension between corporate content moderation policies and free speech principles. The Supreme Court has increasingly grappled with how First Amendment protections apply when private companies wield such extensive control over public discourse.

The anonymity afforded by online platforms has both enhanced and complicated First Amendment protections. While anonymous speech has long enjoyed constitutional protection, dating back to the Federalist Papers, digital anonymity has enabled both protected political discourse and harmful activities like harassment and disinformation. Courts have struggled to balance these competing interests while preserving the essential role of anonymous speech in democratic discourse.

Digital amplification has transformed the reach and impact of individual speech. When the First Amendment was ratified, the practical limitations of communication technologies naturally restricted the spread of information. Today, a single social media post can reach millions within hours, challenging traditional assumptions about the marketplace of ideas and the balance between free expression and other societal interests.

The rise of artificial intelligence and automated content moderation has introduced novel First Amendment questions. When algorithms rather than human editors make decisions about speech, traditional concepts of editorial discretion and prior restraint must be reconsidered. The use of AI to detect and remove prohibited content has raised concerns about both overreach and underenforcement of speech regulations.

Online harassment and cyberbullying have forced courts to reconsider the boundaries between protected speech and unprotected threats or intimidation. While the First Amendment has never protected true threats or incitement to imminent lawless action, applying these doctrines to online communication requires careful consideration of context and intent in digital environments.

The global nature of online platforms has complicated First Amendment jurisdiction. Speech posted online instantly crosses national borders, creating conflicts between American free speech protections and more restrictive international standards. Courts must now consider how territorial limits on constitutional rights apply in cyberspace.

Digital platforms have also transformed religious exercise and establishment clause issues. Online worship services, religious social networks, and faith based apps have created new questions about religious freedom and government neutrality in the digital sphere. The pandemic's shift to virtual religious gatherings highlighted these emerging constitutional questions.

Press freedom has been particularly affected by digital transformation. As traditional media outlets compete with online news sources, blogs, and social media, courts must consider how established First Amendment protections for journalism apply to new forms of digital media and citizen journalism. The rise of paywalls and subscription models has also raised questions about equal access to information.

Commercial speech doctrine has faced new challenges in the digital marketplace. Online advertising, influencer marketing, and targeted commercial content have blurred traditional distinctions between commercial and noncommercial speech. Courts must now consider how First Amendment protections apply to algorithmic advertising and automated commercial communications.

The right of assembly has taken on new meaning in the digital age. Online organizing tools have enabled unprecedented coordination of physical protests while also creating virtual spaces for assembly and association. Questions have emerged about whether digital gathering spaces deserve the same constitutional protection as physical ones.

Encryption and digital privacy technologies have created tension between free speech and national security interests. Courts must consider whether code itself constitutes protected speech and how encryption rights balance against government surveillance needs. The debate over encryption backdoors highlights these competing constitutional interests.

Content moderation policies on major platforms have raised questions about compelled speech and editorial discretion. When platforms are pressured to remove certain content or add warning labels, it implicates both corporate First Amendment rights and user speech interests. The debate over Section 230 of the Communications Decency Act has highlighted these tensions.

The spread of misinformation and disinformation online has challenged traditional First Amendment approaches to false speech. While the amendment generally protects false statements except in specific contexts like defamation, the viral spread of harmful falsehoods has led to calls for reconsidering these protections in the digital age.

Looking ahead, emerging technologies like virtual and augmented reality will likely present new First Amendment challenges. As these immersive technologies blur the line between physical and digital space, courts will need to consider how traditional speech protections apply in these novel contexts.

The evolution of First Amendment rights online demonstrates both the enduring importance and necessary adaptation of constitutional principles in the digital age. While core values of free expression remain vital to democracy, their application must continue to evolve alongside technological change. The challenge for courts and society will be preserving essential speech protections while addressing novel harms and challenges unique to the digital environment.

Privacy Rights: Modern Fourth Amendment

As technology and surveillance capabilities have advanced exponentially, the Fourth Amendment's privacy protections have taken on new urgency and complexity in modern America. What began as a safeguard against physical government intrusion into homes and personal papers now must address digital searches, mass data collection, and emerging questions about privacy in an interconnected world.

The Supreme Court's adaptation of Fourth Amendment principles to digital privacy began in earnest with cases involving cell phone searches. In the landmark Riley v. California decision in 2014, the Court recognized that modern smartphones contain the "privacies of life" in digital form, requiring police to obtain a warrant before searching them incident to arrest. This unanimous ruling signaled the Court's understanding that digital devices require special Fourth Amendment consideration.

Location tracking has emerged as a critical modern privacy battleground. In Carpenter v. United States, the Court held that the government needs a warrant to access cell phone location records, even when they are held by third party service providers. This decision marked a significant shift away from the traditional "third party doctrine," which had held that individuals have no reasonable expectation of privacy in information voluntarily shared with others. The Court recognized that digital technology has made it possible to create a detailed chronicle of a person's movements that would have been impossible when the Fourth Amendment was adopted.

The rise of "smart" devices and the Internet of Things has created new challenges for privacy protection. Internet connected thermostats, speakers, security cameras, and other household devices generate constant streams of intimate data about activities within the home, the space traditionally afforded the strongest Fourth Amendment protection. Courts are now grappling with questions about whether police need warrants to access data from these devices and what standards should govern their use as evidence.

Government surveillance capabilities have expanded dramatically through technologies like facial recognition, automated license plate readers, and drones. These tools enable systematic monitoring of public spaces at a scale previously unimaginable. While courts have generally held that people have no reasonable expectation of privacy in public places, the ability to aggregate and analyze massive amounts of public data to reveal private patterns of life has called this principle into question.

Digital surveillance often occurs without any physical intrusion, challenging traditional Fourth Amendment frameworks focused on physical trespass. Programs collecting bulk communications metadata, for instance, can reveal intimate details about people's associations and activities without ever entering their homes or seizing their physical property. Courts have struggled to apply constitutional privacy protections to these invisible intrusions.

The border search exception to the Fourth Amendment has faced particular scrutiny in the digital age. While authorities have traditionally had broad power to search travelers entering the country, the vast amount of personal data contained on modern devices has led some courts to require at least reasonable suspicion for forensic searches of electronics at the border.

Corporate data collection has complicated Fourth Amendment analysis by creating vast repositories of personal information held by private entities. While the Constitution only restricts government action, the government's ability to access privately held data through subpoenas or voluntary cooperation has raised questions about whether stricter standards should apply when the government seeks to leverage private surveillance.

Encryption and digital security measures have become central to modern Fourth Amendment debates. While encryption provides technical protection for private information, government attempts to mandate backdoors or compel decryption raise novel constitutional questions about self incrimination and reasonable searches in the digital age.

The rise of cloud computing has challenged traditional concepts of location and possession in Fourth Amendment law. When personal files are stored on remote servers, potentially in other countries, courts must determine how constitutional privacy protections apply and what procedures government investigators must follow to access this data.

Artificial intelligence and big data analytics have enabled new forms of predictive policing and surveillance that test Fourth Amendment principles. The ability to use algorithms to identify patterns and predict behavior raises questions about whether these tools constitute searches requiring constitutional safeguards.

The growing use of biometric data like fingerprints and facial scans has created new privacy concerns. Courts have had to consider whether compelling someone to unlock a device with their fingerprint or face is more like providing a physical key, which is generally allowed, or testifying against oneself, which is constitutionally protected.

Social media monitoring by law enforcement has emerged as another frontier of Fourth Amendment law. While public social media posts may not be protected, government use of fake accounts or sophisticated monitoring tools to gather information about individuals and groups has raised constitutional concerns.

Looking ahead, emerging technologies like brain computer interfaces, autonomous vehicles, and augmented reality will likely present novel Fourth Amendment challenges. As technology continues to advance, courts will need to continue adapting constitutional privacy protections to address new forms of government surveillance and intrusion.

The evolution of Fourth Amendment jurisprudence in the digital age demonstrates both the enduring importance of constitutional privacy protections and the need to apply these principles flexibly to new contexts. While the fundamental right to be secure against unreasonable searches remains constant, its application must continue to evolve alongside technological change to maintain meaningful privacy protections in modern society.

Criminal Justice Reform: Modern Applications

The evolution of criminal justice reform has dramatically reshaped how the Constitution's protections apply in modern law enforcement and corrections. While the fundamental rights enshrined in multiple amendments remain unchanged, their interpretation and application continue to evolve in response to changing social values and emerging challenges in the criminal justice system.

One of the most significant modern developments has been the growing recognition of racial disparities in policing, prosecution, and sentencing. Courts have grappled with how constitutional protections can address systemic bias while respecting law enforcement's need to maintain public safety. The Supreme Court's decisions have increasingly acknowledged the role of implicit bias and the need for safeguards against discriminatory practices.

The rise of DNA evidence has transformed both prosecutions and post-conviction proceedings. Courts have had to determine when defendants have constitutional rights to DNA testing and how such evidence intersects with traditional protections against double jeopardy. The ability to definitively prove innocence years after conviction has led to increased scrutiny of finality in criminal judgments and expanded interpretations of due process rights.

Modern interpretations of the Eighth Amendment's cruel and unusual punishment clause have evolved significantly. The Supreme Court has restricted the death penalty's application, particularly for juvenile offenders and intellectually disabled defendants. Questions about lethal injection protocols, solitary confinement, and prison conditions have forced courts to reconsider what constitutes cruel and unusual punishment in contemporary society.

Plea bargaining, now the mechanism resolving the vast majority of criminal cases, has required courts to develop new frameworks for ensuring constitutional rights in a system where few cases go to trial. The Supreme Court has expanded defendants' right to effective counsel during plea negotiations and required clearer disclosures about collateral consequences of guilty pleas.

The treatment of juvenile offenders has undergone particular transformation in modern criminal justice. Courts have increasingly recognized that children are constitutionally different from adults for purposes of sentencing and criminal procedure. This has led to new restrictions on juvenile life sentences and greater emphasis on rehabilitation over punishment for young offenders.

Technology has dramatically impacted modern criminal procedure rights. Body cameras, surveillance footage, and digital evidence have created new questions about defendants' confrontation rights and access to evidence. Courts have had to balance privacy protections with the need for effective law enforcement in an increasingly digital world.

Mental health has become a central focus of modern criminal justice reform. Courts have expanded protections for mentally ill defendants, requiring adequate treatment and considering mental health status in sentencing. Questions about competency to stand trial and the insanity defense continue to evolve as understanding of mental illness advances.

The opioid crisis has forced reconsideration of how constitutional rights apply in drug cases. Courts have grappled with questions about involuntary treatment, drug courts, and the balance between public health and criminal justice approaches. This has led to new interpretations of search and seizure rights in drug cases and expanded consideration of rehabilitation in sentencing.

Mass incarceration has prompted new scrutiny of constitutional rights in corrections. Courts have addressed issues ranging from prison overcrowding to access to medical care, often finding that contemporary practices violate constitutional standards. The human and financial costs of widespread imprisonment have led to broader interpretations of what constitutes cruel and unusual punishment.

Indigent defense remains a critical challenge in modern criminal justice. While the right to counsel is well established, courts continue to wrestle with what constitutes adequate representation given limited public resources. This has led to new standards for public defender caseloads and increased scrutiny of systemic deficiencies in indigent defense.

Asset forfeiture practices have faced growing constitutional challenges. Courts have begun imposing stricter limits on law enforcement's ability to seize property, requiring clearer connections to criminal activity and more robust due process protections for property owners.

Immigration enforcement has raised new questions about how constitutional criminal procedure rights apply to non-citizens. Courts have had to balance immigration enforcement goals with fundamental fairness, particularly regarding right to counsel and protection against self-incrimination in proceedings that blur the line between criminal and civil law.

Restorative justice practices have gained prominence, challenging traditional adversarial models of criminal justice. Courts have had to determine how constitutional rights apply in alternative resolution programs that emphasize rehabilitation and reconciliation over punishment.

The movement for police reform has prompted new interpretations of constitutional limits on law enforcement authority. Courts have revisited standards for use of force, qualified immunity, and police accountability in response to growing concerns about police misconduct and the need for systemic change.

Looking ahead, criminal justice reform continues to evolve as society grapples with questions of fairness, effectiveness, and human dignity in the justice system. Constitutional protections remain vital safeguards, but their application must continue to adapt to address modern challenges and changing social values.

Equal Rights: Modern Fourteenth Amendment

The Fourteenth Amendment's equal protection clause has become an increasingly powerful tool for addressing modern discrimination and inequality. While its origins lie in post Civil War efforts to secure rights for formerly enslaved people, today's courts apply its principles to an ever expanding range of issues involving differential treatment by government entities.

One of the most significant modern applications has been in the realm of gender discrimination. Though the Equal Rights Amendment was never ratified, courts have used the Fourteenth Amendment to strike down many forms of sex based discrimination. The Supreme Court now applies intermediate scrutiny to gender classifications, requiring the government to show an important interest and substantial relationship between that interest and the discriminatory policy. This has led to the invalidation of numerous laws and practices that treated men and women differently without sufficient justification.

Sexual orientation and gender identity have emerged as major frontiers in modern equal protection jurisprudence. The Supreme Court's landmark decisions in cases like Obergefell v. Hodges, which established a constitutional right to same sex marriage, relied heavily on Fourteenth Amendment principles. Courts continue to grapple with questions about discrimination against LGBTQ+ individuals in areas ranging from employment to adoption to healthcare access.

Educational equity remains a critical focus of modern Fourteenth Amendment interpretation. While Brown v. Board of Education established that separate educational facilities are inherently unequal, modern cases deal with more subtle forms of discrimination and inequality. Courts have addressed issues like school funding disparities, tracking systems that create de facto segregation, and access to advanced coursework and special education services.

The intersection of race and criminal justice has prompted new applications of equal protection principles. Courts have had to address claims of racial profiling, discriminatory enforcement patterns, and systemic bias in sentencing. While proving intentional discrimination remains challenging, there is growing recognition of how facially neutral policies can have discriminatory impacts.

Economic inequality has raised new questions about the scope of equal protection. While courts have generally been reluctant to recognize poverty as a suspect classification, modern cases increasingly grapple with how government policies affect different economic classes. This includes challenges to fines and fees in the criminal justice system, access to public benefits, and educational funding models.

Disability rights have expanded significantly through modern Fourteenth Amendment interpretation, often in conjunction with federal legislation like the Americans with Disabilities Act. Courts have recognized that equal protection principles require reasonable accommodations and prohibit arbitrary discrimination against individuals with disabilities.

Immigration status has become another important frontier in equal protection law. Courts have had to balance the federal government's broad authority over immigration with constitutional guarantees of equal protection, particularly regarding access to education, healthcare, and other public services for immigrants and their children.

Voting rights remain a critical area where modern equal protection principles intersect with other constitutional guarantees. Courts continue to address various forms of voter suppression and electoral discrimination, often analyzing them through both Fourteenth Amendment and Voting Rights Act frameworks.

The rise of big data and algorithmic decision making has created new equal protection challenges. Courts are beginning to grapple with how constitutional principles apply when artificial intelligence systems produce disparate impacts on protected groups, even without obvious discriminatory intent.

Access to technology and digital services has emerged as a modern equality concern. Courts have had to consider whether differential access to internet services, online education resources, or digital government services raises equal protection issues, particularly when such disparities fall along racial or economic lines.

Environmental justice has become an important application of equal protection principles. Courts have addressed claims that environmental hazards and climate change impacts disproportionately affect minority and low income communities, though proving intentional discrimination in such cases remains challenging.

Healthcare access and quality have raised significant equal protection questions, particularly during public health crises like the COVID 19 pandemic. Courts have had to address disparities in healthcare delivery, allocation of medical resources, and access to preventive services.

Modern workplace discrimination cases often involve complex intersections of protected characteristics, requiring courts to develop more nuanced approaches to equal protection analysis. This includes addressing multiple bases of discrimination and recognizing how different forms of bias can compound and interact.

Looking ahead, equal protection jurisprudence continues to evolve as society confronts new forms of discrimination and inequality. The challenge remains balancing the amendment's promise of equality with practical limitations on judicial intervention in social and economic policy. Courts must also grapple with how to address systemic inequalities that persist despite formal legal equality.

The modern application of the Fourteenth Amendment's equal protection clause demonstrates both its enduring importance and its adaptability to new challenges. As society continues to evolve and new forms of discrimination emerge, this constitutional guarantee remains a vital tool for promoting equality and combating unjust discrimination in all its forms.

Voting Rights Today: Ongoing Battles

The struggle for voting rights in America continues to evolve, with new battlegrounds emerging even as historical challenges persist. While the Voting Rights Act of 1965 marked a watershed moment in protecting electoral access, recent decades have seen both progress and significant setbacks in the fight to ensure all Americans can exercise their fundamental right to vote.

One of the most consequential developments in modern voting rights was the Supreme Court's 2013 decision in Shelby County v. Holder, which effectively nullified the preclearance requirements of the Voting Rights Act. This decision freed states with histories of discrimination from federal oversight of their election law changes, leading to a wave of new voting restrictions across the country.

In the wake of Shelby County, states have implemented various measures that voting rights advocates argue disproportionately affect minority communities. Strict voter ID requirements have become increasingly common, with supporters claiming they prevent fraud while critics maintain they create unnecessary barriers to voting, particularly for poor and minority voters who may face challenges obtaining required documentation.

Polling place closures have emerged as a significant concern, particularly in minority communities. Since 2013, thousands of polling locations have been shuttered across the country, often requiring voters to travel longer distances and wait in longer lines to cast their ballots. These closures have particularly impacted rural communities and areas with large minority populations.

The practice of voter purges has intensified, with states removing millions of voters from their rolls, sometimes with little notice or questionable justification. While maintaining accurate voter rolls is important, aggressive purge practices have sometimes resulted in eligible voters being wrongly removed from registration lists, forcing them to overcome additional hurdles to exercise their right to vote.

Gerrymandering remains a persistent challenge, with sophisticated computer modeling enabling increasingly precise manipulation of district boundaries for partisan advantage. While racial gerrymandering has been subject to legal challenge, the Supreme Court's 2019 ruling in Rucho v. Common Cause determined that partisan gerrymandering claims are beyond the reach of federal courts, leaving reform efforts to state courts and legislatures.

The rise of early voting restrictions has become another contentious issue. Several states have reduced early voting periods or limited drop box locations, changes that critics argue particularly affect working-class voters who may have less flexibility to vote on Election Day. The COVID-19 pandemic brought these issues into sharp focus as states grappled with balancing public health concerns with voting access.

Mail-in voting has emerged as a major battlefield in contemporary voting rights disputes. While some states have expanded mail voting options, others have imposed new restrictions on who can vote by mail and how those ballots must be handled. Debates over signature matching requirements, ballot receipt deadlines, and witness requirements have led to numerous legal challenges.

Felony disenfranchisement continues to affect millions of Americans, with policies varying significantly by state. While some states have moved to restore voting rights to people with felony convictions, others maintain strict restrictions that voting rights advocates argue perpetuate historical patterns of racial discrimination in the criminal justice system.

Language access remains a crucial issue for many communities. While federal law requires certain jurisdictions to provide voting materials in multiple languages, implementation has been uneven, and many voters with limited English proficiency continue to face challenges accessing the ballot.

The role of money in politics has raised new questions about voting rights and democratic participation. While campaign finance issues are often discussed separately from voting rights, many advocates argue that the outsized influence of wealthy donors effectively dilutes the voting power of ordinary citizens.

New technologies have created both opportunities and challenges for voting rights. While electronic voting systems and online registration can make voting more accessible, concerns about security and reliability have sometimes been used to justify restrictions on voting access. The digital divide also means that technological solutions may not reach all communities equally.

The debate over election administration has intensified, with partisan disputes over everything from voter registration procedures to ballot counting protocols. These conflicts have sometimes led to the politicization of traditionally nonpartisan election operations, raising concerns about the integrity and fairness of the electoral process.

Looking ahead, several key challenges loom large in the voting rights landscape. The need for new federal voting rights legislation remains a major point of contention, with proposals like the John Lewis Voting Rights Advancement Act aimed at restoring and strengthening federal protections. The impact of climate change on voting access is emerging as a concern, as extreme weather events can disrupt elections and disproportionately affect vulnerable communities.

The ongoing battle for voting rights demonstrates that the work of ensuring electoral access remains unfinished. As new challenges emerge and old ones persist, the struggle continues to make the promise of democratic participation a reality for all Americans. The outcome of these current battles will shape the future of American democracy for generations to come.

Amendment Proposals: Current Debates

As the United States moves further into the twenty first century, debates over potential constitutional amendments have taken on new urgency, reflecting both persistent historical concerns and emerging challenges of the modern era. Several amendment proposals have gained particular prominence in recent years, each representing different visions for addressing perceived flaws in America's constitutional framework.

The Equal Rights Amendment (ERA), first proposed in 1923, remains a significant focus of constitutional activism. Despite reaching 38 state ratifications by 2020, questions about expired deadlines and state rescissions have left its status uncertain. Advocates argue that explicit constitutional protection for gender equality remains essential, while opponents contend existing laws provide adequate protections. The debate has sparked renewed discussion about the amendment process itself, particularly regarding Congress's power to impose ratification deadlines.

Campaign finance reform represents another major thread in amendment proposals. Following the Supreme Court's Citizens United decision in 2010, numerous amendments have been proposed to explicitly authorize Congress and states to regulate campaign spending. These proposals seek to address concerns about money in politics, with supporters arguing that unlimited political spending undermines democratic principles. Some versions would declare that corporations do not have constitutional rights identical to natural persons, while others focus specifically on election spending regulations.

The Electoral College has become an increasingly contentious focus of amendment proposals, particularly after presidential elections where the electoral vote winner lost the popular vote. Various proposals range from direct popular election to modified systems that would preserve some federal elements while ensuring closer alignment with national popular will. The National Popular Vote Interstate Compact, while not a constitutional amendment, has emerged as an alternative pathway to reform.

Term limits for Supreme Court justices have gained traction as amendment proposals, particularly as concerns about judicial politics have intensified. Proposals typically suggest 18 year terms with regular appointments every two years, aiming to reduce the stakes of individual nominations and ensure regular rotation on the Court. Critics argue this would undermine judicial independence, while supporters contend it would make the Court more responsive to democratic change.

The balanced budget amendment remains a perennial proposal, though its form has evolved. Modern versions often include provisions for emergency spending and economic downturns, addressing criticisms of earlier proposals. The debate reflects broader disagreements about fiscal policy and federal power, with supporters arguing it would enforce fiscal discipline and opponents warning it could hamstring government response to crises.

Privacy rights have emerged as a focus of amendment proposals in the digital age. These initiatives seek to establish explicit constitutional protection for personal data and digital communications, arguing that existing Fourth Amendment jurisprudence inadequately addresses modern surveillance capabilities and data collection practices. Some proposals specifically address government surveillance, while others extend to corporate data collection.

Voting rights amendments have gained renewed attention, with proposals seeking to establish an explicit constitutional right to vote, ban partisan gerrymandering, or set national standards for election administration. These efforts reflect frustration with court decisions limiting voting rights protections and concern about state level restrictions on voting access.

Environmental protection has emerged as a new frontier for amendment proposals, with various "green amendments" suggested at both federal and state levels. These would establish constitutional rights to clean air, water, and a healthy environment, potentially transforming environmental law and regulation. Critics argue such provisions would be overly broad, while supporters contend they're necessary to address climate change and environmental degradation.

Congressional reform proposals include amendments to change the size of the House of Representatives, modify Senate representation, or establish new procedural rules. Some seek to address perceived democratic deficits in current arrangements, while others aim to break legislative gridlock or reduce partisan polarization.

Proposals addressing presidential power have proliferated, particularly regarding war powers, emergency declarations, and pardon authority. These reflect ongoing debates about executive authority and the balance of powers between branches, often sparked by controversial presidential actions.

The citizenship clause of the Fourteenth Amendment has become another focus, with proposals to modify birthright citizenship rules. These highly controversial proposals highlight ongoing debates about immigration and national identity, though they've gained limited traction in Congress.

Several proposals seek to address specific Supreme Court decisions, showing how amendment proposals often emerge as responses to controversial court rulings. These range from overturning Citizens United to modifying interpretations of the Second Amendment.

The difficulty of achieving the supermajorities required for amendment has led to increased interest in alternative paths to constitutional change, including state level amendments, interstate compacts, and framework legislation. Some advocates have even proposed amendments to modify the amendment process itself, arguing current requirements are too stringent for modern democracy.

The proliferation of amendment proposals reflects both the enduring appeal of constitutional solutions to political problems and the significant barriers to achieving them. While few current proposals appear likely to achieve the required support for ratification in the near term, they serve important functions in public discourse about constitutional values and national priorities. As America continues to evolve, these debates over potential amendments help shape understanding of constitutional principles and possibilities for democratic reform.

Future of Change: Constitutional Evolution

The future of constitutional change in America stands at a critical intersection of tradition and transformation, as evolving social needs and technological advances create new pressures on the nation's fundamental law. While the amendment process remains deliberately difficult, requiring broad consensus across diverse constituencies, the mechanisms of constitutional evolution continue to adapt to modern challenges.

Digital technology presents perhaps the most significant catalyst for future constitutional change. As artificial intelligence, virtual reality, and quantum computing reshape human interaction and capability, questions about fundamental rights and governmental powers take on new dimensions. Future amendments may need to address not just privacy rights, but the very nature of human autonomy in an age of algorithmic decision making and neural interfaces.

Climate change and environmental degradation pose another crucial challenge that may drive constitutional evolution. As the effects of global warming become more severe, pressure may mount for constitutional provisions establishing environmental rights or reforming federal powers to address planetary scale threats. The traditional framework of state and federal authority may require adjustment to handle challenges that transcend not just state but national boundaries.

Demographic shifts will likely influence future amendment efforts as well. As America becomes increasingly diverse and urbanized, questions of representation and voting rights take on new urgency. The current constitutional structure, designed for a primarily rural eighteenth century society, may require updating to reflect modern population patterns and ensure equitable representation across communities.

Economic inequality and technological disruption of traditional employment may drive reconsideration of constitutional economic rights. Future amendments might need to address questions of universal basic income, digital currency, or rights to education and healthcare that weren't contemplated by the original framers. The nature of property rights themselves may require reexamination in an age of intellectual property and virtual assets.

The mechanisms of amendment may themselves evolve. While Article V's basic framework has served well, new technologies could transform how amendments are proposed and ratified. Digital platforms might enable more direct citizen participation in the amendment process, while maintaining necessary deliberative safeguards. Some scholars envision blockchain technology providing secure, transparent systems for constitutional revision.

Global interconnection will likely influence future constitutional development. As international law and transnational governance structures evolve, amendments may be needed to clarify the relationship between domestic and international legal frameworks. The traditional concept of sovereignty itself may require updating for an age of global challenges and instantaneous worldwide communication.

The role of states in the amendment process may shift as well. While state ratification remains fundamental, interstate compacts and regional cooperation might provide new models for constitutional evolution. Some envision a future where states serve as laboratories for constitutional innovation, testing new approaches before national adoption.

Artificial intelligence and automated systems pose particular challenges for constitutional evolution. Future amendments may need to address questions of algorithmic fairness, robot rights, or human agency in an automated world. The fundamental concepts of personhood and citizenship that underpin constitutional rights may require reconsideration as technology blurs traditional boundaries.

The pace of change itself presents challenges for constitutional evolution. While the deliberate nature of the amendment process provides important stability, rapidly evolving technology and social conditions may require more responsive mechanisms for constitutional adaptation. Finding the balance between stability and adaptability remains crucial.

The future may see increased emphasis on positive rights alongside traditional negative liberties. As society grows more complex and interdependent, amendments might establish affirmative governmental obligations in areas like education, healthcare, or environmental protection. This would represent a significant evolution from the Constitution's original focus on limiting government power.

Space exploration and development could drive novel constitutional questions requiring amendment. As human activity extends beyond Earth, new frameworks may be needed for property rights, governance, and human rights in space. The very concept of territorial jurisdiction that underlies much constitutional law may require rethinking.

The evolution of human consciousness and capability through technology might necessitate constitutional adaptation. As neural enhancement, genetic modification, and human machine interfaces become reality, fundamental questions about equality, rights, and human dignity may require constitutional attention.

Yet amid all this change, the core principles of democratic governance, individual rights, and the rule of law remain crucial. Future amendments will likely build upon these foundations while adapting them to new circumstances. The challenge lies in preserving essential constitutional values while enabling necessary evolution.

The role of citizen engagement in constitutional change may expand through technology and social innovation. New forms of deliberative democracy might emerge, enabling broader participation in constitutional dialogue while maintaining necessary safeguards against hasty or ill considered changes.

Whatever specific changes emerge, the process of constitutional evolution will continue to reflect the dynamic tension between stability and adaptation that has characterized American constitutionalism from the beginning. The future of constitutional change lies not in abandoning traditional principles, but in thoughtfully applying them to new challenges while maintaining the democratic legitimacy that gives the Constitution its enduring power.

Citizen Power: Grassroots Amendment Efforts

Grassroots movements have always been the true engine of constitutional change in America, transforming passionate civic engagement into lasting legal reform. While the formal amendment process requires action by Congress and state legislatures, the real power has consistently come from ordinary citizens organizing to demand change.

The history of successful amendments reveals a consistent pattern of bottom-up activism preceding formal legal changes. The women's suffrage movement spent decades building support through local organizations, protest marches, and public education campaigns before the Nineteenth Amendment was ratified. Similarly, the civil rights movement's grassroots organizing and direct action created the political pressure that led to voting rights protections in the Twenty-Fourth and Twenty-Sixth Amendments.

Modern grassroots movements continue this tradition while adapting new technologies and organizing strategies. Social media and digital platforms enable rapid mobilization and information sharing, allowing amendment campaigns to quickly build nationwide networks of supporters. Online petitioning and crowdfunding help grassroots groups compete with established interests in shaping the constitutional conversation.

The Equal Rights Amendment movement demonstrates both the persistence and evolution of grassroots constitutional activism. Though the ERA fell short of ratification in the 1970s, grassroots organizers kept the cause alive through decades of setbacks. Modern ERA advocates combine traditional tactics like marches and lobbying with sophisticated digital organizing and legal strategies, maintaining pressure for constitutional gender equality.

Climate change has sparked new forms of constitutional activism, with youth-led movements demanding constitutional provisions for environmental protection. These campaigns often link local direct action with global networks, recognizing that constitutional reform must address planetary-scale challenges. Their innovative tactics include climate strikes, artistic protests, and strategic litigation pushing courts to recognize environmental rights.

Economic justice movements increasingly frame their demands in constitutional terms, calling for amendments to address wealth inequality and corporate power. Groups advocating for amendments to overturn Citizens United or establish economic rights build broad coalitions linking local community organizations with national reform networks. They often combine traditional organizing with sophisticated policy research and legal advocacy.

The power of grassroots constitutional activism lies in its ability to transform abstract legal principles into concrete human stories. Successful movements help citizens see how constitutional changes affect their daily lives, building emotional investment in abstract reforms. Personal testimonies, community forums, and local organizing create the human connections that sustain long-term amendment campaigns.

Digital democracy has created new opportunities for citizen participation in constitutional dialogue. Online forums enable widespread public discussion of proposed amendments, while citizen journalism and social media allow grassroots voices to challenge established narratives. Some movements experiment with digital tools for collaborative amendment drafting, seeking to make the process more participatory.

Yet effective grassroots campaigns still require old-fashioned organizing skills. Building trust through face-to-face relationships, developing local leadership, and maintaining long-term commitment remain essential. The most successful movements combine digital innovation with proven organizing methods, recognizing that technology alone cannot create lasting change.

Education plays a crucial role in grassroots constitutional activism. Successful movements invest heavily in public education, helping citizens understand both existing constitutional provisions and proposed changes. They develop accessible materials explaining complex legal concepts and train community members to serve as constitutional educators.

Coalition building across different movements and constituencies remains vital for amendment campaigns. Modern grassroots groups often link seemingly separate issues, showing how various constitutional reforms connect to broader struggles for justice and democracy. This intersectional approach helps build the broad support needed for successful amendments.

Youth leadership has become increasingly prominent in constitutional activism, with young organizers bringing fresh perspectives and tactics to amendment campaigns. Their facility with digital organizing and comfort with bold systemic changes energizes traditional movement structures. Youth-led campaigns often emphasize long-term vision while maintaining urgency for immediate action.

Local government engagement offers another avenue for grassroots constitutional impact. City councils and state legislatures can become laboratories for testing constitutional ideas and building momentum for national changes. Local resolution campaigns help build grassroots power while creating pressure for broader reforms.

The challenge for modern grassroots movements lies in maintaining long-term commitment while responding to immediate crises. Successful amendment campaigns typically require years or decades of sustained effort, yet modern attention spans and news cycles favor short-term actions. Building organizational structures that can sustain long-term campaigns while remaining responsive to current events becomes crucial.

Looking forward, grassroots constitutional activism seems likely to become even more important as complex global challenges require democratic responses. The combination of traditional organizing wisdom with modern technological tools creates new possibilities for citizen-driven constitutional change. The future of American democracy may well depend on ordinary citizens continuing to exercise their power to reshape their fundamental law.

Democracy's Promise: Amendment Legacy

The legacy of constitutional amendments in American democracy reveals a profound truth: the Constitution's greatest strength lies not in its permanence, but in its capacity for change. Through 27 successful amendments, Americans have repeatedly demonstrated their ability to reshape their fundamental law to meet new challenges and expand democratic participation. This evolutionary capacity has helped the Constitution remain relevant and legitimate across more than two centuries of dramatic social transformation.

Each amendment tells a story of democratic awakening and citizen empowerment. The abolition of slavery through the Thirteenth Amendment marked America's delayed but decisive break with human bondage. Women's suffrage via the Nineteenth Amendment partially fulfilled the promise of universal citizenship. The voting rights amendments steadily dismantled barriers of race, wealth, and age that had restricted democratic participation.

These changes didn't just expand rights on paper they fundamentally transformed American society and consciousness. The Fourteenth Amendment's guarantees of equal protection and due process provided the legal foundation for civil rights advances that would have been unimaginable to the founding generation. The First Amendment's protections for free speech and assembly enabled the very movements that would push for future constitutional changes.

The amendment process itself embodies democratic principles by requiring broad consensus across different levels of government and regions of the country. While this high bar has prevented many proposed amendments from succeeding, it ensures that successful changes represent genuine national agreement rather than temporary majorities. The difficulty of the process has generally produced careful deliberation and enduring reforms.

The amendments' impact extends far beyond their specific provisions. They establish broader principles that courts and citizens draw upon to address new situations. The Fourth Amendment's prohibition on unreasonable searches now shapes debates about digital privacy. The First Amendment's protection of press freedom applies to online journalism and social media. This adaptability allows constitutional principles to remain relevant in changing times.

Perhaps most importantly, the amendments demonstrate that ordinary citizens can successfully change their fundamental law through peaceful democratic processes. This legacy of orderly constitutional change has helped America avoid the violent upheavals that have plagued many other nations. The knowledge that the Constitution can be amended provides a peaceful path for addressing deep societal conflicts.

The amendments also reveal an expanding conception of democracy and rights. Early amendments focused primarily on limiting federal power and protecting specific individual liberties. Later amendments increasingly emphasized expanding democratic participation and ensuring equal treatment under law. This evolution reflects America's gradual progress toward a more inclusive and egalitarian understanding of democracy.

The impact of constitutional amendments often unfolds over decades through court decisions and changing social attitudes. The Fourteenth Amendment's full implications for racial equality weren't realized until the civil rights movement of the 20th century. The First Amendment's robust protection of political speech emerged gradually through decades of Supreme Court decisions. This process of interpretation and implementation continues to shape how amendments affect American life.

Failed amendment efforts also leave important legacies. The Equal Rights Amendment campaign fundamentally shifted public attitudes about gender equality even without achieving ratification. Movements for amendments addressing issues like balanced budgets or congressional term limits have influenced political debates and policy changes even when falling short of constitutional change.

Looking at the amendments collectively reveals recurring themes in American constitutional development. The steady expansion of voting rights reflects a persistent drive toward broader democratic participation. Multiple amendments addressing presidential succession and disability show ongoing efforts to ensure stable executive leadership. Amendments dealing with federal power and individual rights demonstrate the continuing tension between national authority and personal liberty.

The amendments also highlight the role of crisis and conflict in constitutional change. The Civil War amendments transformed American federalism and citizenship. The Sixteenth Amendment enabling income tax and the Seventeenth Amendment providing direct election of senators emerged from Progressive Era reforms. The Twenty Fifth Amendment addressing presidential succession followed John F. Kennedy's assassination.

Yet the amendment legacy suggests that successful constitutional change requires more than just crisis it demands sustained organizing, careful coalition building, and strategic timing. Amendments succeed when they address widely recognized problems with solutions that command broad support. The repeal of Prohibition via the Twenty First Amendment succeeded because the problems with the Eighteenth Amendment had become overwhelmingly clear.

The amendments demonstrate both the durability and adaptability of the American constitutional system. Core principles established in 1787 remain intact, while significant changes have been achieved through orderly democratic processes. This combination of stability and flexibility has helped the Constitution maintain its legitimacy across dramatic social transformations.

Modern challenges from climate change to artificial intelligence may well require future constitutional amendments. The amendment legacy suggests that successful changes will require broad coalition building, careful drafting, and clear connection to fundamental democratic principles. The capacity for constitutional evolution remains essential to American democracy's future.

Understanding this legacy of constitutional change is crucial for citizens seeking to protect and expand democratic rights today. The amendments remind us that the Constitution is not a static document but a living framework that each generation must help shape. They stand as testament to the American people's capacity to transform their fundamental law through democratic means.

The People's Document: Conclusion

In concluding this examination of America's constitutional amendments, we return to the essential truth that the Constitution belongs to the people. While lawyers and judges interpret its provisions, and politicians debate its meaning, the power to fundamentally reshape this document has always rested with ordinary citizens working together for change.

This democratic ownership is evident in the remarkably diverse coalition of Americans who have successfully amended the Constitution. From abolitionists and suffragettes to civil rights activists and youth voters, amendment campaigns have united Americans across regional, racial, class, and partisan divides. These movements demonstrate that constitutional change, though difficult, remains achievable when citizens organize effectively around compelling causes.

The twenty seven ratified amendments tell a story of gradual but persistent progress toward a more inclusive democracy. The expansion of voting rights through multiple amendments transformed a system initially limited to property owning white men into one promising universal adult suffrage. Protections for individual rights have grown from the original Bill of Rights to encompass new understandings of liberty and equality. Even amendments addressing technical matters like presidential succession reflect democratic efforts to ensure stable and accountable government.

Yet the amendment process has done more than just add new provisions to the Constitution. It has fundamentally shaped American political culture by establishing peaceful constitutional change as an alternative to violence or revolution. When faced with profound societal conflicts, Americans have repeatedly chosen the challenging path of amendment rather than abandonment of constitutional government. This commitment to working within the system while simultaneously striving to improve it represents a unique contribution to democratic practice.

The amendments also reveal the remarkable adaptability of the American constitutional system. The basic framework established in 1787 has proven capable of accommodating dramatic social and technological changes through careful amendment. From enabling income tax to protecting digital privacy rights, amendments have helped the Constitution remain relevant in a rapidly evolving world. This flexibility, combined with the stability provided by the difficult amendment process, has enabled the Constitution to maintain its authority across more than two centuries.

Perhaps most importantly, the amendments demonstrate that constitutional change comes not from legal experts or political elites but from organized citizens demanding reform. Every successful amendment began with people recognizing problems and working together to address them through constitutional means. The amendments are thus a testament to democratic agency the ability of citizens to reshape their fundamental law through peaceful collective action.

This popular foundation gives the amendments particular legitimacy and durability. Unlike changes imposed by judicial interpretation or legislative action, amendments approved by supermajorities of Congress and state legislatures represent genuine national consensus. While the meaning of specific provisions may be debated, the democratic legitimacy of the amendment process itself remains widely accepted.

The amendments also highlight the crucial role of civic education and engagement in constitutional democracy. Successful amendment campaigns have required citizens to understand their constitutional system deeply enough to change it effectively. This necessity has helped create an informed and active citizenry capable of meaningful democratic participation. Today's citizens inherit this responsibility to understand and engage with their constitutional system.

Looking forward, the amendment process remains vital for addressing contemporary challenges. Issues from campaign finance reform to privacy rights may well require constitutional solutions. The experience of past amendments suggests that successful changes will require broad coalitions, careful drafting, and clear connection to fundamental democratic principles. The difficulty of the process helps ensure that only well considered and widely supported changes succeed.

The amendments remind us that the Constitution is not a sacred text to be worshipped but a practical framework for democratic governance that can and should be improved when necessary. They stand as proof that ordinary citizens working together can reshape their fundamental law to better serve democratic ideals. This capacity for peaceful constitutional evolution may be the American system's greatest strength.

Understanding this history of constitutional change is crucial for citizens today. It provides both inspiration and practical lessons for those seeking to protect and expand democratic rights. The amendments demonstrate that while constitutional change is difficult, it remains possible when citizens organize effectively around compelling causes. They remind us that the Constitution's power and legitimacy ultimately rest not with courts or politicians but with the American people themselves.

The story of America's constitutional amendments is thus fundamentally a story of citizen power and democratic possibility. It reminds us that the Constitution is not just a historical document but a living framework that each generation must help shape. Through twenty seven amendments, Americans have repeatedly demonstrated their capacity to improve their fundamental law through democratic means. This legacy of peaceful constitutional evolution remains essential to meeting the challenges facing American democracy in the twenty first century and beyond.

Don't miss out!

Visit the website below and you can sign up to receive emails whenever James R. Whitfield publishes a new book. There's no charge and no obligation.

https://books2read.com/r/B-A-DDLUC-EXBIF

BOOKS 2 READ

Connecting independent readers to independent writers.

www.ingramcontent.com/pod-product-compliance
Lightning Source LLC
LaVergne TN
LVHW090357210926
848480LV00002B/372
* 9 7 9 8 2 3 0 0 3 4 8 9 6 *